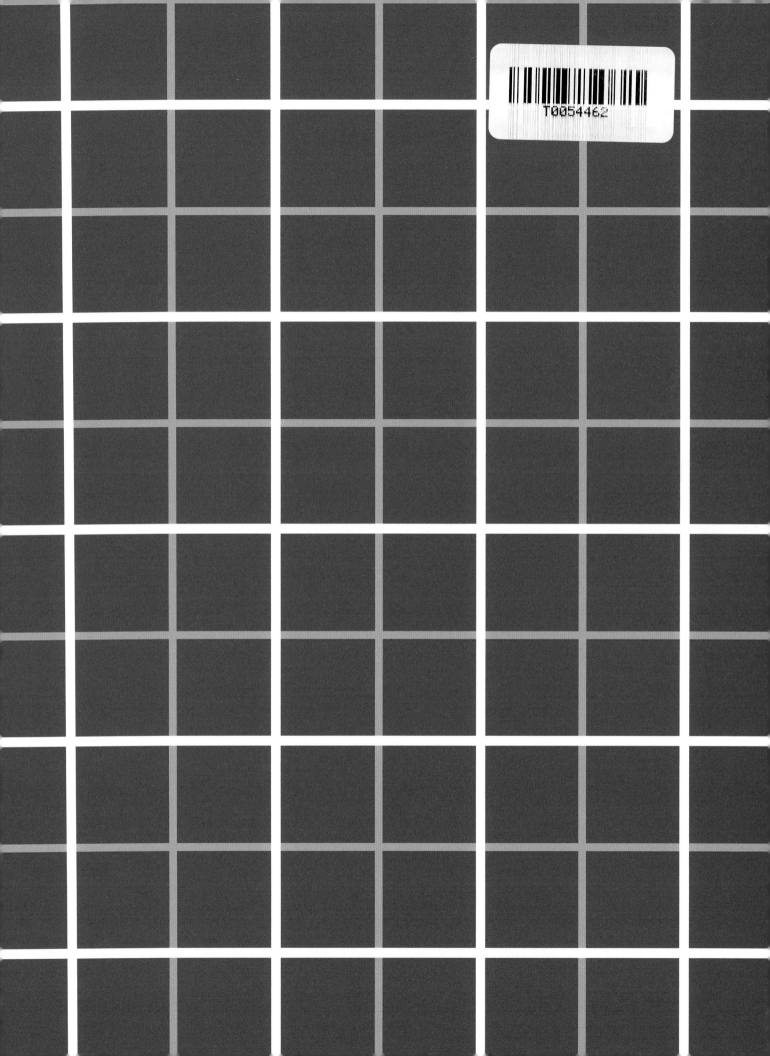

T0054462

Decorate Happy

Decorate Happy

BOLD, COLORFUL INTERIORS

ANTHONY BARATTA

Written with Antonia van der Meer

RIZZOLI
NEW YORK

New York · Paris · London · Milan

Table of Contents

INTRODUCTION

People's lives are like colorful quilts—all of the crazy pieces eventually come together to form one amazing, beautiful whole. No one's life story is a simple beige blanket. In my opinion, homes shouldn't be either. Ideally, your living space should reflect the energy and light that is uniquely yours. If it doesn't, it's time for a change. Head forth immediately in search of a place full of life and love and color and playfulness.

I want you to be fearless when you decorate your home. That's why I wrote this book. I am hoping that my enthusiasm for color and pattern and bold American style will ignite a sense of excitement and possibility in you. Being fearless is invigorating! I hereby give you permission to break out of the boring and to surround yourself with happiness. I want you to live in rooms that smile.

Decorating homes is pure joy for me. With thirty-nine years of exuberant design behind me and (hopefully) many, many more exciting years ahead, I can't imagine any other life for myself. Of course, it took me a while to get where I am today. Years ago, when I left my home in Nutley, New Jersey, and set out for Fordham University in New York City, I thought I wanted to become an architect. But first, I decided to major in art history at Fordham—a decision that I can't thank myself enough for making. It exposed me to art theory and gave me an increased social, historical, philosophical, and cultural understanding of the world around me. Among other things, I learned never to underestimate the impact that our visual surroundings can have on us.

I fell in love with many of the artists I studied in college, such as Andy Warhol, Roy Lichtenstein, Ellsworth Kelly, and Jasper Johns. I was drawn to their strength of color, the graphic quality of their work, and the freshness that they bring to every canvas. You can see the roots of my design in their art. But I have always been particularly fond of Henri Matisse—he has probably influenced me more than any other painter. A French artist, he blasted into the twentieth century with never-before-seen flattened forms and heightened colors. He threw perspective out the window and ran on instinct. Soon known as one of the Fauves (the "wild beasts") of his artistic generation, he had a cheerful creativity that could not be denied. I admire that wildness and endeavor to take his spirit of fearlessness and joy with me into my own designs. Whether I'm working on a spacious mansion or within the limited confines of a small city apartment, I make sure to pack in a ton of personality and color. I hope Matisse would be proud!

While at Fordham, I was lucky enough to intern at one of the greatest museums in the world: The Metropolitan Museum of Art. For some reason (maybe I had a particularly trustworthy face), the Met let me wander anywhere and everywhere I wanted. It was glorious. I felt like I had the keys to the kingdom. I explored from the basements to the attics, and one day I stumbled upon a group of marvelous cast-plaster versions of Roman sculptures. I never forgot them. Later in life, I began collecting them, and now some are on display in my house on Long Island. We all have seminal moments like this in our lives. Everything from our past gets filed away and influences who we become and how we react to things.

I remember, for example, vacationing in the Adirondacks with friends when I was a kid. We stayed at a Great Camp, the rustic yet elegant escapes built during the Gilded Age, now so hard to find. I don't think it had any heat, and we slept in drafty wooden cabins that smelled of evergreen trees and wildflowers. That trip still influences my work to this day. I'm sure it's at the root of my attraction to folk art and my fondness for the rustic. It pops up everywhere: take, for example, a formal dining room for a house I designed in Utah—I put birch bark on the walls in lieu of wallpaper. At the beginning of my career, some people thought folk art had no place in high-end design, but I always knew its early-American charm would be perfectly at home mixed with classic European elegance.

I also was influenced by a trip to Williamsburg, Virginia, when I was only nine years old. I think that may have been the first moment I realized I might want to be a designer. I was fascinated by the details in the Governor's Palace—the arched doorways, intricate woodwork and tray ceilings—and fell in love with the place.

When I graduated from college, my life took an unexpected turn. I ended up getting an internship with the late Bill Diamond, one of the greatest American interior designers. Eventually this became a partnership, and Bill and I worked together for more than thirty years. I was so lucky to have had Bill as my partner; he was a true leader and creative force in design. To this day he influences my work, and I try to channel his genius. Now I get to continue on my design path, building on all the great things we did. I work to reinvigorate the classics, reimagine the traditional, and tweak the modern and contemporary designs that are popular now. I am constantly learning and expanding the ways in which I express myself.

If you're wondering what happened with that architecture degree, I didn't get it. I loved what I was doing with Bill so much that I stayed with interior design. Rest assured, however, I never lost my love for architecture. In fact, I am happiest when I am involved with a project

The design for the plaid wallpaper came from a favorite flannel shirt of mine. There's something about enveloping a room in fabric that keeps a room cozy and warm. This was the perfect feeling for a house in Deer Valley. The room also features a red Victorian chair which is a signature piece. It may seem out of place in a ski house until you remember Deer Valley's history as a silver mining town back in the late 1800s. I'm constantly trying to relate decorating to the place and time. The chair is a subtle reminder of the town and its roots.

from the ground up—literally. I want to be there for the start of construction! Most architects don't design with the furniture in mind; that's not what they are trained to do. I have the whole picture in my head when I work on something, right down to imagining an alcove for a grandfather clock or the sweep of a staircase. The excitement comes from having the ability to do both at the same time—architectural and decorative work.

Fast-forward to today: my design work is deeply entrenched in classic American style, which is at the root of everything I do. Sometimes that means anchors and sailboats and nautical chic. I've loved them since I was a little boy. American style can also manifest itself as a giant red barn door for a home's entrance. It may lead to a custom-made birch bed, a table twisted to life from twigs, or a hooked floral rug on the floor. It may have the historical importance of centuries past, or it may veer into the pop art world, with mod rooms and bright primary colors. American decor also honors classic styles, like chintz, and soft colors, like pretty pinks and blues. I am proud of being an American designer and standing up for all that includes.

Throughout my years as a designer, I have learned to embrace many styles. I decorate for clients with very different tastes, sensibilities, lifestyles, and locations. I grow from every experience. I borrow from the past and mix things together a new way the next time. I value all the schemes and themes I've done before and continue to build upon them. In this book, I will take you to all the places I've decorated and elevated: the ski lodges, country homes, seaside retreats, and penthouses. Each one shines in its own way.

Although they are all unique, they share one consistent underpinning: they exude happiness. To decorate happy, let your home be an extension of yourself and look for things that bring you joy. Appeal to your sense of humor when you decorate. Be playful. Include things that make you smile. Allow for exuberant self-expression. Above all, look to color. I think that color is everything. That's because to be colorful is to be full of life and good cheer. Color can be controversial, carefree, animated, stimulating, and evocative, but never dull. I'm particularly delighted by red and blue, both of which I use a lot. I'll never get tired of red. It clears my head and brightens my day!

I also take pleasure in pattern. Plaids, houndstooths, windowpane checks, stripes, florals, geometrics, and argyles—I adore them all. You see them recur in much of my work, sometimes as pattern on pattern. Primary colors and geometric shapes lift me up and make me happy.

For a mudroom, a multi-functional bench was created for a family that prides itself on being tidy. I love mixing a tattersall plaid wall covering with a checkerboard fabric on the bench. I am not afraid to place all manner of plaids together—ginghams and plaids and checkerboards. It's part of my pattern lexicon.

To decorate happy, let your home be an extension of yourself and look for things that bring you joy.

So what makes *you* happy? How do you want to decorate *your* home? Think about it.

Every home paints a picture of the people who live in it. In New York City, I have a groovy little bachelor pad. In Westhampton, I've created a glamorous black, white, and tan retreat. In Williamsburg, my eighteenth-century brick house is filled with the historical richness of Americana. There are many ways you can express yourself: your choices of art, fabric, furniture, fashion, or paint color. You can also inject personality through something as small as a crystal doorknob or a clever doorstop.

I always ask my clients, Where's the fun? Life is too short for staid or stodgy. I want you to smile and enjoy the things around you. I want you to be excited about the red plaid fabric on a chair, cheered by the nautical brass compass on a table, heartened by the colorful braided rug in front of the sofa, and delighted by the delicate blue vase on the mantel. People have this idea that decorating a home means reaching for perfection. Not at all! Trying for that kind of flawlessness makes a room stiff. I do not design stage sets. I design for *living*.

I decided I wanted to write this book to help people find their way to a truly happy home. I want to ignite your passion for decorating. I hope it helps you to embrace happiness in every aspect of your life.

The homes in this book reflect the diversity of real people's hobbies and enthusiasms—for nature and art and cooking and sailing and skiing and entertaining. These homes represent the many and varied routes to personal happiness. In this book, I tell all their joyful stories, house by house, in bold American style. I hope to hear your story someday.

OPPOSITE: Black-and-white striped wallcovering provides a striking backdrop for a unique mix of antiques and vintage finds in my shop in Westhampton Beach.

MOUNTAIN MAGIC

Nothing is more beautiful than a red door. As you step through this magical portal, you enter a special place. I knew the floor of the entry would take a lot of abuse, so I used stone. The same stone paves the outside of the house. It's the idea of the outside coming in. A lot of weather comes into this house when the door is opened! But I didn't use stone everywhere, because the house is also a cozy place and I want you to be able to walk around in your socks.

When my clients first contacted me about decorating this big, gorgeous mountain home for them, I knew it would be a stunner. The location is spectacular. The views are achingly beautiful. It simply doesn't get better than this. In the world of skiing, Utah wins best in show. One thing was certain: the architecture and decor of this ski home in Deer Valley would have to match the superlatives that are routinely showered upon this fabled resort: unforgettable, award-winning, luxurious, glamorous, exclusive, and world-class. For every delight you are met with outside the house, I would need to find its match inside. That's a tall order for a decorator, but I was energized from the start. Big American country houses are a joy to work on, and this one had everything going for it right from the start.

There are some assignments where I can immediately see all that it can be from the very beginning. The minute I saw the site for the house, I knew exactly what this stellar place would look like. I imagined a happy confluence of richly colored patterns, from plaids and ginghams to tartans and Fair Isle–sweater patterns. I conceived a strict color palette of bright reds, dark greens, and deep blues. The idea was to avoid cutesy Americana and to instead have a bold, tailored look. I bought furniture and decorative objects at auctions and antiques shows to give the house authenticity and character. These items were augmented by possessions from the clients' own collection.

As a designer, I was competing with a huge, majestic mountain. You want to respect that enormity and be sure everything is to scale. Take, for example, the red-and-black hunter's plaid in the great room, the giant blue-and-white squares on the kitchen floor, the red quilt-like tiles in the

I adore big American country homes—they are one of the true joys of my work as an interior designer.

bathroom, and the lederhosen-green leather chairs in the dining room. Each one is a showstopper and can stand up to the beauty and prowess of the mountain outside.

I almost always start out by designing the biggest room in the house. Here, that was the great room, so named because of its cathedral ceilings and magical views of the Deer Valley peaks. It can be tricky to decorate a room of this height and scale. I sought out oversize ingredients: a big quilt on the wall, a giant rooster sculpture, bold plaids and windowpane check fabrics, a powerfully patterned rug, and plenty of seating.

A ski house is a unique thing. Those who come back to this house want to relax and recover from the day's outdoor activities. Cold, wet, and tired, they want to be warmed and coddled. Entering this home feels like you're being wrapped in a soft flannel blanket. As with most modern ski houses, the floors are heated and there are boot warmers. I made sure the sofas in the great room are longer, deeper, and higher than the average couch to welcome tired bodies back from the slopes.

I wanted everything to feel appropriate to ski country. This is not a downtown loft. It should not be wiped clean of references to skiing. On the contrary, I added continual reminders of where you are and why, starting with the massive red front door, which takes the barn door to the next level. This is an entryway into a holiday world. There are stone floors for slushy foot traffic.

For the great room, I mixed plaids, windowpanes, quilts, and woolens. The rooster sculpture by Mark Perry on the mantel was the first thing I bought for the house. It says a lot about the direction of my thinking. It's big, it's oversize, it's high-style. It's super modern, but it's also folk art. That's everything about the house all rolled into one piece.

Inspiration came from ski resorts around the world: lederhosen colors, Fair-Isle–sweater patterns, wools, tartans, and plaids.

There's a ski room that, while highly functional, is as well designed and perfectly decorated as any other room in the house.

There are references to other ski resorts, including nods to the Poconos in Pennsylvania, where I first skied as a kid, with its rustic charm and woodsy decor, but this house is not only about American decorating. It's a notch higher than that. I referenced places worldwide, from Switzerland to Italy to Austria. I borrowed details from European ski chalets: warm woods, gingerbread trim, and flower themes. I wanted a mashup of every winter wonderland there is.

The master bedroom is one of the coolest rooms in the house. It has a very special view. You can't compete with that, but you can try to keep pace with it. The room's decor is bold and intensely patterned. The wallcovering takes the idea of a flannel shirt and dresses up the whole room in its coziness. Even the ceiling is covered in flannel, blanketing the space in its soft warmth. The reason it doesn't feel overwhelming is because I used white beams to break it up. The chimney around the fireplace is also painted white to create breathing space.

A strict color palette and classic patterns like stripes and plaids contribute to a sense of longevity. The end result is a home that will stand the test of time. Twenty years from now, it will still be good-looking.

The great room is like a crazy quilt of wonderful fabrics and patterns. The repeating hunter's plaids are always part of my work. Here, in black and red, they are perfect for the space. The red ottoman fabric was inspired by a Fair Isle sweater, and the hooked rug on the floor is done in a folksy quilt pattern. At the same time, the rug is reminiscent of a Navajo blanket. It has a Western vibe. A big room can hold a lot of pattern.

This ski house is a
fantasy. It's a big
playpen in the snow.
I wanted it to be
happy, fun, and playful.
Floor-to-ceiling
windows open up the
great room to the great
outdoors. That's what
everyone is here for.

The dining room has a whimsical stag fabric on the walls. I couldn't resist! The wine cabinet is made of birch and hickory and bottle glass. The dining room must be versatile enough for activities from formal dinners to casual après-ski parties. Below the chair rail, the wall is covered in the skin of a birch tree. This gives the room a rustic, natural feel. The juxtaposition of rustic with formal furniture is just the ticket. There are elegant moments in the dining room, too, such as the large, traditional antique English table. The chairs are the colors of lederhosen, done in suede on one side and a woven wool plaid on the other.

The generous kitchen has a slate gray–and–red theme. It feels like a Swiss chalet. The diamond-shaped quilt pattern on the backsplash behind the stove continues to carry the folk-art theme through the house. On the floor, I chose a large diamond pattern, then distressed it because I didn't want it to look all shiny and new. Floors need to be worry-free in a ski-house kitchen.

A sprinkling of snowflakes magically appear on a braided rug for a touch of whimsy.

The breakfast nook was a place to explore layers of pattern. The plaid rug with the braided border has a snowflake overlay. It's as if there were recently a fresh snowfall. After the red band, I kept going with additional rings around the rug. When things are custom, you can flex your muscles and try new things. The chair covers add another pretty layer, and the table is made partly from an industrial piece. FOLLOWING SPREAD: Repurposing things is always part of my design work. On the left, an early industrial machine part plays a new role in this ski house as a mirror in the entryway. On the right, an antique dry sink is turned into a vanity in the powder room, and a blue-and-white mixing bowl becomes a basin. The mirror above the vanity was taken from an old carnival ride. You never know where you're going to find a treasure!

Each guest room has a different color and vibe. Here, the room is Austrian-themed, with custom-made black four-poster beds and an engaging pattern on the wall that somehow reminds me of a cuckoo clock. The red plaid of the rug is oversize, the headboards are red-and-white gingham, and the benches at the foot of the bed were repurposed from antique buggy seats. This is the girls' room, and I wanted it to have a more feminine look. I think Liesl and Louisa von Trapp would feel comfortable waking up in this room! FOLLOWING SPREAD: The master bedroom has an elegant, rustic feel, with walls covered in a felted flannel plaid designed specifically for the project. When mixing patterns I start with strong geometrics like the checkerboard and the plaids, then add florals. White woodwork provides balance. The palette is a simple, straightforward trio of red, gray, and white.

LEFT: The guest room is decorated in pine green with a striped carpet. The antique Empire chest with folk arrows looks like a camp chest. OPPOSITE: The bed is a new take on a traditional American four-poster, done here with an upholstered headboard. The turnings are more contemporary as well. The lamps in the room are made from antique fire extinguishers. They have a wonderful, rustic patina to them. It adds something clever and humorous to the room.

ABOVE: In the master bath, an American quilt pattern and Russian fabric prints mix together to create a cheery room. The traditional tub has a prime view. The vanities and doors are made from antique cherry, which looks lovely against a freshly painted white wall. OPPOSITE: The guest bathroom has pine tree wallpaper. The clawfoot tub is surrounded by a bay of windows dressed in casual relaxed sloop shades that soften the linear reality of the room. The evergreen rug pattern is reminiscent of the Swiss flag, a nod to another famous ski location.

FOUR FEARLESS DECORATING IDEAS

INDUSTRIAL PIECES FILL THE BILL IN LARGE SPACES. I love to use giant industrial cogs and other pieces in residential decor. This works especially well in big country homes. Anytime you have a cavernous space to fill, industrial pieces can help. Not only do they match the size and scale, they also add character and age. Don't be afraid to combine seemingly disparate objects, like a polished-wood tabletop with an old iron machine part as a base.

HEAVILY PATTERNED ROOMS NEED BALANCE. The balance comes from having the right weight distribution of big patterns and small ones. The master bedroom, for example, might seem over-the-top, but I used a lot of restraint and control to achieve the look. Most of the room is covered in a single big pattern. All the other patterns in the room quiet down to mesh with the bigger one. The more muted checkerboard pattern on the carpeting recedes.

STONE IS A FORGIVING MATERIAL. Stone flooring can take a lot of abuse. Over time, it will retain its good looks. If you have a high-traffic area or live in a place where a lot of weather tends to come into the house every time you open the door, consider it for your entry. As an added benefit, it has a nice shine and tone that spiffs up any entrance and gives character to your floor. No two pieces are ever exactly alike because it is not a manufactured material.

JUXTAPOSE THE RUSTIC WITH THE FORMAL. There's something wonderful about the meeting of traditional, sophisticated European furniture and plainer, somewhat unsophisticated pieces. The rural and the urban mix quite nicely. The homespun feeling of natural, rustic touches helps to warm the colder formality of more elegant furnishings. In return, the formal helps to elevate the folksy. I like finding that balance.

Most ski rooms are just functional: a place to drop off skis, hang up coats, and step out of ski boots. They're usually an afterthought. Not here. This room is as highly designed and as delightful as any other room in the house, with lots of entertaining ski motifs. Even the woodwork on the wall, which looks like a picket fence, is actually a row of little wooden skis.

SAILOR'S DELIGHT

The wood floors are all painted white, and the wainscoting goes most of the way up the wall, leaving only a little space for the chocolate-brown wallpaper to peek out. I love seeing that taste of color above the white. Everything in the house reflects the history of the sea, from the vintage mermaid paintings to the whales—even the backs of the English chairs look like ships' wheels. The dioramas of sailing vessels at the top are inset sixteen inches into the wall, for a perfect three-dimensional museum-quality feel.

A home should always be a true reflection of a client's passions and personalities. That's what makes it a happy place to be. The family that resides in this spectacular house on the Long Island Sound in Rye, New York, loves to sail. They spend lots of time on the water, and their heart is tied to the sea. I wanted to channel that embrace of all things coastal into my design concept. At the same time, I had no intention of making it into a typical beach house. Instead, when coming to this project, I thought to myself, If I were a sea captain, how would I like to live? Surrounded by nautical charm and my collected treasures, of course! The design feels unabashedly American to me, deeply embedded in a New England style of life, even though I incorporated British, Portuguese, and even Moroccan pieces along the way. (I like to imagine that the sea captain behind this house visited many parts of the world.)

Part of the challenge of decorating this house was finding a spot for everything the family had collected over the years, such as the pair of wooden whales that hang in the entryway, the nineteenth-century moss-green chest that's the star of the show under the staircase, or a collection of nautical transferware on the mantel above the fireplace in the living room. If you're patient, everything eventually finds its way to the perfect place. The client has an extensive collection of folk art, paintings, and collectibles that represent a life well lived, and I had a lot of fun honoring that.

Each item in the house speaks of the sea, from stitched compass points on an ottoman to anchor sconces on a wall. Even the window treatments in the living room are a conscious nod to boating: they remind me of the sail of a boat. The nautical rope wallpaper in the entryway makes a strong statement. It has a delicious chocolate-brown background that complements the olive greens, reds, and gray-blues used

There's a richness to a home by the sea. The nautical collectibles are true treasures.

throughout the rest of the house. The kicker comes from reversing the pattern inside the arch as you head up the staircase. Showing the flip side of a pattern is always successful—it gives the theme dimension and breaks up the rhythm in a good way.

Unique, handcrafted, idiosyncratic furniture and fabrics fill the house: drop-leaf tables, wing chairs, Sheridan chairs, crewel fabrics, and hooked rugs, for starters. There's lots of mahogany and faux mahogany that gives the home a decidedly eighteenth-century feel. Americans have always had a love affair with painted furniture, and I'm a member of that club. It has the ability to add a happy, homey feel to any room. In the end, I used everything at my disposal—from high-style to country—to create this cozy captain's mansion.

The architecture of the 1930s also influenced my design. That's when the house was built, and there were curved staircases and arched doorways, big fireplaces and bay windows. These are classic, traditional elements. But I find that the fine and the folksy can mingle together quite nicely. The colorful braided rug on the stairs, a recurring theme in my work, adds charm and dials down the formality of the house. A playfully preppy vibe is splashed throughout with the use of lots of plaids and florals.

The maritime marvelousness extends to the bedrooms and baths. But in those rooms the energy relaxes a bit, with mellower hues and softer patterns. In one child's bedroom, there's a captain's bed and plenty of room for the ribbons and trophies won in sailboat races.

Through the sun-filled bay windows, there is a view of either blue water or verdant nature. Whether the family is enjoying themselves inside the house or outside—it's the perfect place to relax and appreciate the rewards of living by the sea.

A striped runner on the front stairs introduces you to almost every color in the palette: reds, blues, greens, and browns. The entry floor is left bare, allowing the white-painted wood to shine. A dark chest of drawers looks like the perfect place for a sea captain to stash his trinkets and papers.

In the living room, decorated mainly in reds and blues, a sand-colored rug is like sherbet after a rich meal. It cleanses the palette in a room that has lots of bright color saturation. The rug is a very geometric Portuguese needlepoint, and it feels almost like a stencil on the floor. The fabrics are floral, plaid, and windowpane patterns, creating a homey mix of familiar favorites.

I never get tired of a red room. It warms the soul and has lasting appeal.

White floors and wainscoting offset vermillion-red walls in the dining room. It's said that the color red is good for the appetite—if that's the case, people should eat well here! A round mahogany table and ladder-back chairs are as traditional as it gets, but the tassels on the yellow seat cushions are anything but predictable.

The kitchen and breakfast nook are sunny spots, made more so by glass cabinets, white countertops, and cozy captain's chairs with floral seat cushions. The round braided rug includes rings of brown, blue, green, and red.

If there's one touch from this house that people remember, I'm guessing it would be this reverse-printed wallpaper, as seen through an arch on the stairway. It's a showstopper. White on brown or brown on white, it's reminiscent of fishing nets. I like to think of this motif as the freshest catch of the day.

A wooden four-
poster bed lends
romance to the sea
captain's story. The
white bedding has
just a touch of frills
and all the elegance
of swirly monograms.
A pink wing chair
always makes
a fine bedfellow.

LEFT: The bathroom
benefits from jaunty red
and white stripes.
OPPOSITE: The girl's room
is an architectural delight
of arches, built-ins, and a
captain's bed.

LEFT: The deck is perched on a quiet inlet off Long Island Sound, and looks out over a spectacular nature preserve. The house feels far away from it all, even though some days the New York City skyline is visible in the distance. OPPOSITE: The key to the family room is its unique color combination: saturated raspberry pink on the sofas, a custom-woven chocolate brown tartan on a rattan settee and chair, and the lime green trim on the window dressing.

FOUR FEARLESS
DECORATING IDEAS

DEFY CONVENTION. Who says that high-style antique furniture can't coexist with braided rugs and country quilts? Regency-era dining chairs lose some of their stuffiness and get a fresh update with kicky plaid seat cushions. I even adorned them with cheerful tassels. Sure, the chandelier above the dining table is formal and glamorous, but the entire room doesn't have to march to the same beat. What's interesting is the mix. That's when a room transforms from ordinary to special.

SPREAD THE WEALTH. Beautiful collectibles should be spaced out throughout the home. Don't try to force them all into the same room, the same cabinet, or the same curio. This house is like a treasure hunt, leading you on a pleasurable, meandering path to view all its maritime wonders. Visitors can take their time and enjoy each item along the way, never feeling overwhelmed by the entire nautical art collection.

CELEBRATE SCREENED PORCHES. I am always happiest when a house has a screened-in porch. This is one of the best places to sit and enjoy the sea breezes and the fresh scent of the stately green trees outside. Long Island Sound has its own special vibe, and there's no better way to take it all in than here, where the light is magnificent and you are close to the water. Wicker furniture always works on a porch, especially when it's Victorian. I chose a gray-green color to mirror the nature preserve and bay that the porch overlooks.

REMEMBER: CREWEL RULES. Crewelwork is a type of embroidery, and it can lend so much unique personality and life to a room. The technique has been around forever and widely used for centuries in India and Greece. Seventeenth-century British royalty loved it in their bedrooms. And it's still irresistible today! The embroidery is done using woolen yarns on a cotton, linen, jute, silk, or velvet fabric. The yarn is how crewel differs from regular embroidery, which is done with thread. Crewel is chunkier and fuller, and it has a very textural appearance and feel. The embroidered motifs are often flowers or wildlife. The great thing is that you can use crewelwork anywhere, from window treatments to upholstery for chairs.

Say hello to this incredible high-backed Victorian wicker chair. It deserves a salute. Surrounded by floor-to-ceiling windows, a model sailboat with a plaid sail (of course!) dominates the porch and reminds you that this is a home for sailors.

OPEN HOUSE

Small outdoor spaces can have a big impact, especially when you add a waterfall. The blue, green, and white glass tiles beautifully reflect the serene colors of the ocean. To complete the picture, I wanted the floor to look like cool, clean cement— perfect for a warm-weather home. But cement can crack, and it sometimes doesn't wear well, so faux-cement ceramic tiles provided the perfect solution. Oversize thirty-inch squares give it a smooth feel.

One of the best things about color and pattern is the way in which they can transform a home. I absolutely love taking an unassuming profile and giving it an infusion of pop and panache. My goal is always to create a happy space, and I know no better way to do that than with bold hues and strong graphics. This newly refurbished getaway in Fort Lauderdale, Florida, is an energetic surprise among a row of more formulaic, mid-1960s houses. And that suits its owner perfectly.

I've had a lot of experience with these low-slung, single-story dwellings. There is so much that can be done to a ranch house that upgrading them is a piece of cake. And decorating the interior with colorful, graphic verve is the icing on that cake.

It was very clear from the beginning that the low roofline and too many interior walls were holding this gem of a house back from its true potential. To start, we ripped out the core and lost all the separate rooms that were weighing down the design. The owner wanted a more loftlike feel, so we completely opened the back of the house with floor-to-ceiling windows and added a charming courtyard space in the front. The house was off to a good start, but we reached for new heights by raising the ceilings. When you have the chance to improve upon the architectural design of a property, do it. An extra sixteen inches of height in the living room makes a big difference. Now light pours in through the floor-to-ceiling windows and the house feels connected to the outdoors.

When I step back and look, the whole design reminds me of an Henri Matisse painting with its modern, flat perspective. The unconventional French artist's work inspires me to make rooms that are colorful but not overcooked. By that, I mean a

You can see the entire color palette for the house in the living room. Because it's a central space, I wanted to incorporate every color we had: red, blue, orange, and turquoise. They all look so good together, especially when they are mixed with tan and white. I was also inspired by the graphic nature of the Ji Zhou work of art placed over the cream sofa. It hangs on a feature wall covered in blue linen and pulls the whole space together.

When working with dynamic patterns, there must never be chaos. Everything in the house needs to stay within a consistent palette.

design that doesn't try too hard. The colors in this ranch house are beautifully balanced. A Matisse painting is perfectly clear. It's not a stretch to understand it. I always want my homes to have that simplicity and clarity.

Of course, my work is always all about color. Color is everything! It brings joy to a house. The same hues should run through every room, creating a complete picture, like the perfect painting. Turquoise is a great Florida shade, but it looks even better when paired with orangey reds—I used a lot of those shades here. Adding tans and whites helps to give those brighter colors the space they need to really shine. Meanwhile, I splashed tons of white paint on the walls. I almost always do. White brings a crispness to the whole design.

Patterns are wonderful, but it's tiring to have only intensely geometric lines in a room. The graphic concept needs to be softened, as it is here with a deep blue, kidney-shaped Vladimir Kagan sofa that's curvy and fluid. The little white end tables add a lyricism with their rounded edges. There's an unexpected elegance to these sculptural shapes, especially when set against the bold, graphic rug that is featured.

LEFT: The vintage Saporiti Italia chairs cut a dashing figure around the white dining table. And what better way to rev up the energy in the room than with a fun racing stripe on the teal fabric? I love adding these playful touches. **OPPOSITE:** In the kitchen, the blue theme continues with cabinetry and Norman Cherner counter stools. A porthole window brings the light in.

Like Matisse, I love pattern.
And pattern on pattern.

I've built my career on being adventurous, and I know how to create drama with pattern and scale. A house like this demands it. Modern, sculptural furnishings are right at home here. There are certain forms that I love and employ over and over. When I bring them into a house, it's like bringing an old friend with me. Who can say no to a bright red Eero Saarinen Womb chair or a reproduction of a classic Vladimir Kagan sofa—two musts for the living room? There are jazzy stripes and graphic lines throughout the rooms, but there are many spots for the eye to rest as well. Follow the line of the curvaceous sofa or look up to see the circles of ring lights hanging from the ceiling. I also added a pair of natural leather Milo Baughman–inspired chairs to the mix. I often like to add natural leather: it says quality, it offers a hint of masculinity, and it adds an element of surprise. But the best thing about the living area may be the dynamic round rug of patterned lines that showcases every color in the home's palette. It grounds the whole room.

Luckily the owner of this wonderful home had a lot of patience, and he came to the project wanting a fun experience. He had great enthusiasm for the design work, and he was very open to new ideas—the ideal client always is. A good design ends up saying a lot about the person who lives there. This is his vision of the world. He wanted to be surrounded by color and happiness, and I think that's what we achieved.

The master bedroom has a screened wall with big shutters for privacy. As an added benefit, they give the scale of the windows a boost, making them appear taller than they are. The headboard is my design, using three different fabrics in broad horizontal stripes. The braided rug is modern and fresh, and it mirrors the headboard, including every color from the home's overall palette. The '60s pendant lights give a nod to nautical style.

Decor can be dialed up or down, such as a quiet houndstooth, a bold stripe, a muted solid, or a vibrant hue.

I always love incorporating art with sailboats into my designs. In this case, the client already owned these two little gems, and we framed them in white and hung them on a patterned blue-gray wallpaper. Of course, I never miss an opportunity to dress up a bed with colorful pillows. The bold stripes play quite nicely with the houndstooth wallpaper.

In the lanai kitchen, the muted dining table purposely recedes and disappears, making the wonderful patterned tiles behind it the focus. I drew the design first on paper, and then we turned my drawing into a giant mural with tiles. I love the Latin influence in this screened room and the Brazilian style. It reminds me of Miami. Because it opens to the pool, it's a great place for entertaining.

FOUR FEARLESS DECORATING IDEAS

LET THE SUNSHINE IN. When in doubt, open out. There's a big, bright world out there. Embrace it. Light and air make a home a joy to be in, whether for work, for play, or for rest. Floor-to-ceiling windows overlook the pool off the lanai kitchen. Without them, the house would feel much darker and less open. When you let the rays in, you let happiness stream in as well. That's a place people want to be!

RESPECT THE LOCATION. When designing and decorating a home, always think about where it is situated. Whenever you can nod to your surroundings, you should. Your home is a part of the world around it. You chose its location for a reason, and your love for the area should be honored somewhere in the interior design. Fort Lauderdale is best known for its glorious sandy strands, quiet boating canals, and proximity to the Everglades. Paying homage to that was a must. I created a waterfall in the front courtyard to provide the gentle, soothing sound of the sea that everyone loves.

MAKE ART A PART OF YOUR VISION. I hate to say it, but one misplaced painting can wreck a design. It can be very difficult for a designer to work solely with a client's existing collection of artwork. It's wonderful when someone is willing to expand his or her collection to match the aesthetic of the house. The owner of this ranch was very open to that idea, and he came with me to Art Basel in Miami Beach, a major show for modern and contemporary works. Together, we discovered what he liked and what would work in his home. If you can, work with a good art adviser. It's best to get insight from someone who knows more than you do. You'll not only expand your artworks, you'll also expand your mind.

CREATE A PLAN AND STICK TO IT. I don't take twenty pieces of furniture, throw them up in the air, and see where they land. You can't get crazy. Everything must be carefully considered. In a way, I like to think of all the perfectly placed design elements throughout a home as a map, with all roads leading to the greater design concept. I do this by moving from one room to another with the same repeating themes. In one room, a certain color or pattern has a starring role. In another, the same color or pattern is just an accent. The mix of furniture is done the same way. Contemporary pieces and modern pieces appear throughout the house.

A cheerful blue-and-white striped rug leads your eye straight out to the curvy backyard pool and lush, landscaped greenery. Everything on the screened porch reminds you that this happy home is in the Sunshine State. The outdoor white-leather chairs feel like snappy little sails, and the geometric pillows provide the perfect punctuation marks on a sleek oyster white sofa.

RUSTIC ROMANCE

Texture plays a huge role in making this house homey and comfortable. Hard, sleek, or shiny surfaces are out; warm, romantic fabrics are in. They're wonderfully welcoming and what the world could use more of right now. Visual comfort comes from a snug-looking red-and-turquoise quilt that hangs from the rough-hewn wood boards of the cabin wall. An austere white wooden bench gets cozy with the addition of a blue-and-white needlepoint cushion. The brightly colored braided rug warms up a painted floor with its beautiful colors and fabulous feel.

This resort home was created to reflect the specific joys, hobbies, and interests of one very special owner: a nature photographer who raises butterflies and loves to spend time outdoors, canoeing on the lake and walking with her two loyal golden retrievers. The woods are a magical place for her, so I decorated these cabins with great respect for Mother Nature and the wonderful escape she provides us.

The house tells a vibrant story in every room. The beauty and charm of these cabins in the woods depends in large part on its history and location. Built in the early 1900s, it has all the authentic attributes of the great camps of that period. It's an integral part of its surroundings, with a tidy boathouse for sunny days and a rustic lean-to with a firepit for cool nights. The owner is so happy being here that she now lives year-round in what is called the Winter House—the only dwelling on the grounds with heat. The Summer House and the boat house and other cozy, casual sleeping quarters around the property are used only seasonally.

The design spins easily from rugged to whimsical, with great respect for the flora, fauna, and wildlife of the camp's majestic Adirondacks setting. Because butterflies are the owner's passion, we made them a key feature, from quilts to wall murals. Using her expert knowledge, the owner personally directed our decorative painter to include the specific species she wanted. Monarch butterflies, of course, are known for their orange colors. Other butterflies can also display amazing shades of turquoise, blue, green, and yellow. Color, so much a part of nature, was obviously going to be at the heart of this house, from a signature Diamond Baratta bold red wing chair and a bright blue quilted ottoman to a pastel turquoise

I have a fondness for the rustic. It's simple perfection to be tucked away in a wooden cabin surrounded by tall trees and wildflowers.

grandfather clock and a light pink coverlet on one of the beds. The lighthearted white-birch bed designed by master furniture maker Paul Flammang is unique and delightful. The hand-painted butterflies on the bedroom walls, done by David Cohn, and the colorful braided rugs on the floor in every room call to mind the gingerbread houses of youthful fairy tales.

Among all the stories this house tells, though, my favorite is the one about the evolution of my design. I'm very proud of the way classic Baratta reds and turquoises are used in unique ways. As a designer, it's not always necessary to reinvent the wheel. The continuum is much more interesting to me. I try to avoid falling into the trendy trap; instead, I use what has been successful in the past and add extra layers to it every time in a way that satisfies me. I had worked with this owner before on her other homes in the Hamptons and in New York City, but it was time to move ahead with a fresh twist on all the things she had appreciated about my previous work. My creative director, Erick Espinoza, took a lead role on this project. With a love of what had come before, he took this home to the next level with a fresh vision for the future of Anthony Baratta design.

OPPOSITE: Traditional Adirondack chairs are a must for the outdoor areas, but we made these standard bearers even more comfortable by adding soft red-and-white striped cushions. FOLLOWING SPREAD: A beautiful turquoise, hand-painted grandmother clock looks like it could be in a chalet in Switzerland as easily as in a cabin in the Adirondacks. A carved wooden "Black Forest" bear hoists a bouquet of fresh flowers. It's fun to show things with character and stories behind them.

Red and turquoise make happy companions.

Inside any of these rooms, you lose yourself in the tall tales told by the many folk-art quilts, patchwork upholstery, and charming vintage finds. The collected and curated decor pays homage to the homespun, woodsman-esque character of a mountain compound, with items like a staghorn console table with antlers, a massive stone hearth, and rough tree-trunk beams across the living room ceiling. Follow the bread-crumb trail to find the animals and flowers depicted in the large squares of the custom-made rug in the living room. The rug is what started it all and it is the heart of the room. The owner personally picked out all the animals and plants that would be incorporated in its pattern.

The rooms contain a delightful blend of American folk art, Victorian pieces, European antiques, and modern furnishings. It works because we keep the enthusiastic mix happening throughout the house. A lot of design tries to be much more serious; we came to play. A lively plaid chair from the mid-1980s has no problem sharing the space with a modern ceiling fan or an elegant pair of hand-painted Delft vases. Everything can't be campy in a camp!

The Adirondacks is a magical place of great adventure, and this house spins a yarn that definitely doesn't disappoint.

A signature Baratta red wing chair is the star of the show in a room full of turquoises and royal blues. This home displays an interesting combination of formal furniture moved here from the owner's apartment in Manhattan and the more comfy, casual digs traditionally found in a simple camp-like setting. Every inch of the living room displays something of interest—a tall Victorian lamp, a nineteenth-century coal podium with lift-up lid, a surprising hexagon-shaped end table, a collection of earthenware in a curio. You could never get bored here!

PREVIOUS SPREAD: **The room explodes with our passion for pattern.** LEFT: **The ottoman steals the show— if that's possible—with a crazy quilted compass design on top.** OPPOSITE: **On a nearby club chair, white needlepoint houses stand out against a red background. A little Swiss chalet charm works well in the room. We painted the wood ceiling a pale blue- green to give the eye a rest and make sure the room wasn't too woodsy.**

The birch bed looks as if it has been pulled from a fairy tale—full of sweet dreams of flowers and pine cones. A pair of antique Dutch wall sconces made from pressed metal flank the headboard. A brightly colored quilt—one of many the client collects—rests at the foot of the bed.

LEFT: **A** small rustic wood sign outdoors welcomes visitors to **Butterfly Camp** and signals home for the owner. Great camps deserve great names. OPPOSITE: **I** love big, local signs like this one, proudly announcing the Adirondack location. FOLLOWING SPREAD: **T**his wood lean-to takes glamping to the max! It's so peaceful outside in the woods and on the water.

FOUR FEARLESS
DECORATING IDEAS

EMBRACE THE OLD. Victorian furniture is part of my signature. I love how its lines are bold and strong and have great curves. It symbolizes happiness for me. I use it in the most modern and most historic houses. Starting from scratch by buying all-new furniture for a house is the surest way to end up with a home that looks like a hotel lobby, and no one wants that. Instead, surround yourself with lovingly curated antiques, folk art, and vintage finds—the things you treasure. They add character that newer, trendier pieces can never match.

PAINT YOUR FLOORS. A wooden staircase under a runner needn't be plain. Let it shine with personality by giving it a coat of paint, like the teal color we used on the steps. The staircase is then topped with a colorful braided runner. If color is good, more color is even better! Painting your floors adds warmth and brings a sense of fun to a room.

FIND ONE THING THAT BECOMES YOUR SIGNATURE STYLE—WHETHER IT'S A RED WING CHAIR OR A NEEDLEPOINT CHAIR. These are things to be treasured. When you are creating your own home, look for those objects and furnishings. Is there something in your decorating that will always be associated with you?

TASTEFUL TOUCHES CAN GO ANYWHERE. And there's nothing more tasteful than a pair of classically beautiful blue Delft vases. Place them on a fireplace mantel, and they always work. You see them make an appearance in almost every house I work on.

A sleeping porch with a hanging bed is paradise on a warm summer night. Screens all around make sure mosquitoes don't ruin the experience. The blue-painted floors are all the decoration needed—nature does the rest.

COUNTRY CLASSIC

A table lamp created from a blue-and-white Chinese vase sits on a wood table with a marble top. Much of the furniture is Louis XV– and Louis XVI–style. Upholstered blue linen on the living room walls adds an elegant touch. The blue-and-white windowpane rug was inspired by an eighteenth-century French wallpaper. You can find inspiration for patterns everywhere: expand your search beyond Google, look in beautiful art books, and collect pictures of the concepts you love. If you do the research and hang on to those classic looks, your pattern choices will never look dated.

When my clients took me to see their large Connecticut country house situated on a vast estate, I was wowed. It had coffered ceilings, bay windows, and lots of strong American architectural elements. Even better, it had a charming one-hundred-year history: the structure was originally used as a carriage house in the early twentieth century.

Carriage houses are typically separate outbuildings belonging to a main house on a large estate. This one was probably built to store horse-drawn buggies and all the tack and related equipment. Back in the day, the coachman would often live on the second floor. Because of its unique storage needs, the space inside these houses tends to be cavernous and open. Over time, of course, the structure changed. Horses and carriages became things of the past, and people began to use the space for living. There were renovations and additions that increased the size and function of this house substantially before my clients ever came along.

Even so, the proportions and scale of the rooms are unusual and dramatic. I realized right away that the grand, oversize spaces would demand that I think big—really big. Like an artist with an enormous canvas to cover, I knew that I would need to use bold, broad strokes.

As grand as the home is, however, at its heart it will always be a country house. Nodding to that, I opted for wide-plank wood floors throughout, braided rugs, and hand-painted chests—all things that feel authentically rural. I also selected colors with real country flavor, and the result is a very pretty palette of barn red, moss green, cornflower blue, and golden yellow. In some rooms, we played up the golden yellow. In other rooms, it was the blue or the green that got a chance to shine.

LEFT: **A blue-painted Swedish chest looks as if it came from an old farmhouse, and yet it is right at home topped with large white Grecian-style urns. The wallpaper is the big draw, however, with its repeating pattern of classic Wedgwood-style cameos. The Wedgwood blue color has been reinvented with a slightly different hue so that it has its own personality.** OPPOSITE: **I often use striped runners on steps, but here I was drawn to a nubby braided pebble pattern. Notice the handrails, done in a blue lacquer paint for an unexpected style boost. The wide-plank wood floors help maintain the country-house feel amid the high-style furnishings.** FOLLOWING SPREAD: **The mantel was original to the room, as was all the woodwork. The rug pattern was taken from a nineteenth-century French wallpaper and it has a strong country house look.**

"I have a fearless use of color."

That's the fun of having a palette like this. You can use all the colors but dial them up or down in each area to create a whole new look. Blue was the predominant shade in most of the rooms, though. Blue in a country house reminds me of wildflowers like irises, blue columbines, Queen Anne's Thimbles, and mayflowers. Just as blue flowers wake up a garden, blue in a country house stirs feelings of contentment.

The blue path through the house starts in the entryway. The first thing you see is a beautiful wide staircase, which offers a gracious introduction to the home. There were so many things that could have been done here, but we chose a Wedgwood pattern for the walls. I've always loved Jasperware pottery with its unglazed matte finish. The cameos are universally known and adored, but we recolored them to move away from the classic Wedgwood blue toward a hue that's a little brighter and livelier.

With the house in mind, I set out for Argentina to shop. Buenos Aires, in particular the San Telmo neighborhood, has a treasure trove of French furniture that I knew would be perfect for the space. I scooped up lots of fifteenth- and sixteenth-century antiques and reproductions that seemed to be crying out for a place in the Connecticut manse. Mixing in rustic pieces with the more formal furniture helps keep that country-house vibe alive, and I'm always drawn to handmade things because no two are ever exactly alike. The pieces did not all have to be formal, fancy, or fine; they just had to be signature items, like the dining room chairs. It's so beautiful to have French chairs embroidered with a flower basket on the seats. The cane-back chairs help tone things down and stop the upholstery from becoming overwhelming.

I used one of my all-time-favorite fabrics in the living room. Bill Diamond and I created this pattern, called "Julietta," for Lee Jofa, and it was inspired by an eighteenth-century decorative screen. The red colorway provides a powerful backdrop for the hand-painted birds

PREVIOUS SPREAD: In front of a sun-filled window there's nothing better than a charming antique French daybed, or lit de repos. OPPOSITE: The dining room is a deep dive into blue, and I find it very beautiful. I adore the blue-and-white lattice-patterned wallcovering and matching window treatments. The design on the rug is raised, which adds dimension and warmth. For the rug, I reversed the pattern. While the wallcovering has a light background, the rug has a deep blue background with a white relief. It's intense, but I love it. Heavy-duty color and pattern saturation like this can work extremely well. It satisfies the soul, like a rich dessert.

LEFT AND OPPOSITE: A classic blue-and-white checkerboard floor is emblematic of my work. The house is a perfect mix of homespun country style and fancier European furnishings. This assemblage is unique. There are Scandinavian, French, Italian, and British influences. The botanicals, reverse-painted on glass, underscore the feeling that this house is like a magnificent bunch of handpicked wildflowers.

"Red, yellow, and blue lend true country flavor to the house."

and flowers and cameos. Because of all the wonderful patterned fabrics we used throughout on the comfy upholstery, we kept the curtains simple. In most of the rooms, the window treatments are all white with a leading edge done in French-style embroidery. Those little details are extremely important—never forget about the edging! From a sweet little French bench with botanicals to the églomisé on the refrigerator door, this home is filled with these touches.

In the den, things got a little more casual and clubby—no florals here. I wanted this space to read more masculine, so I chose plaid, plaid, and more plaid. The pure focus in this room is the walls. I like when you walk into a room and know exactly what you're looking at. The strong pattern grabs your attention, and you just want to hang out here with a lively conversationalist or a good book.

The master bedroom, by contrast, became a more elegant, private retreat. The sheer size of the room was a little daunting, but there's nothing like toile to make a cavernous room look cozy. The patterns are all pretty but subdued. The moss green is very restful. I like that two vastly different spaces—the den and the bedroom—can coexist in the same house. The house is big enough to handle it. Besides, it's not very exciting if every room in your home has the exact same theme or look.

From its more humble beginnings as a carriage house to its current position as a country mansion, this home has never lost its character or forgotten its past. The new interior decoration has only amplified its distinctly beautiful qualities, and that's what I'm most proud of.

A painted Austrian chest says country house to me. The skirted matching chairs are supremely comfortable, and the yellow-and-white checked curtains are a fun addition. The vertical simplicity adds a little needed height to the room. The crazy quilted sofa is a conversation starter—it was handmade piece by piece by a quilter. When I work with an artist, I give them lots of free rein to create what they envision. My trust in them always pays off, like it did here. The rug brings us back to the red, one of the strongest colors in the house. It was inspired by a vintage bandanna pattern.

Nothing evokes a library like a clubby plaid. Using the same fabric on the sofa, walls, and windows gives it strength and simplicity simultaneously. The wicker chest doubles as a coffee table, but it looks like something you would take with you on a hot air–balloon ride. **FOLLOWING SPREAD:** The soaring cathedral ceiling demands a wallpaper that will make the master bedroom feel a little cozier. I chose a pretty moss green toile to bring you back down to earth. The antique French furniture and tole lamps had to be oversize to look good in the space.

In the spacious bathroom, I used tiles to create a look that resembles wallpaper. This pretty pictorial is framed by a classic arch over the tub with pilasters, and a corresponding arch frames the door. The tiles are from Portugal and match the blue colors of the house. The result is so charming and inviting; this bathroom has undeniable style and grace. I am always very careful when choosing a bathtub, as they can easily give away the date of a project. Keep your fixtures classic or they will soon look passé. The vanities and matching medicine cabinets are all classic white, with details that mirror the architectural pillars on the wall. Everything is very symmetrical. On the limestone floor, small squares of color and pattern maintain interest.

FOUR FEARLESS
DECORATING IDEAS

AVOID MUSHINESS. What do I mean by mushiness? A mushy room has only one note—all florals, for example. It's nice to start with a lovely floral, but you need to build on that, not repeatedly copy it. Add a lively check or a cheeky plaid to the room. Then think about introducing a stripe. Throw in a small pattern. And don't forget to invite lots of solids to the party. That's my recipe for design success. (In answer to your question: Yes, there is a method to my madness!)

PUT FABRIC ON YOUR WALLS. What can I say? I have an aversion to Sheetrock. It doesn't speak to quality in a room, and it leaves me cold. I'm a big fan of linen on walls because it's warm and cozy. It adds texture and interest in a way that mere paint cannot always do. Also, fabric has an added benefit because it can hide flaws. Architectural problems? Cover them with fabric. Using fabric on your walls is an excellent way to add another pattern to the room. In this home, I opted for a plaid on the walls of the den and a Wedgwood pattern in the front hall. There's much more room to play when you open yourself up to the idea of captivating wallcoverings.

KNOW THAT ONE IS NOT THE LONELIEST NUMBER. I prefer an interesting, organic selection of furnishings to matchy-matchy sets. If I find an antique chair that I want for a room, I don't fret if there is only one available. It doesn't matter to me if there is a pair or not. You can always use similar forms and fabrics to create the idea of a pair without locating an exact match. In fact, I often like it better that way.

BLUE-AND-WHITE POTTERY MAKES GREAT LAMPS. If you look at my work, you'll see lots of Chinese vases and Delftware being used as table lamps. You can't go wrong with big blue-and-white pottery as lighting. I'm not interested in teensy-weensy lamps; lamps should be done on a big scale. My preference is always for a pleated lampshade. And while I am on the subject, lamps are highly preferable to canned lighting in the ceiling. Poking holes in your ceiling every few feet makes it look like Swiss cheese. I hate it. Instead, surround yourself with the warm lighting from gorgeous decorative lamps. You can thank me later.

An eighteenth-century French chair with an embroidered flower basket on the seat is a charming addition to the rosy wood of a classic Louis XVI dining table.

ROMAN HOLIDAY

The entry's wallpaper is a brick pattern inspired by a floor in Milan. The palette I used throughout the house begins right here: camel, black, and white. I am often creatively energized by something that I later tweak to suit myself. My dining room chairs, for example, were inspired by a boudoir chair whose shape appealed to me. I designed something similar by making the same form bigger so that it would work as a dining room chair. I have a set of eight, and I spread them around the house. They appear in all different locations, but they can come together when I have company for dinner. A plaster bust of Hercules sits near the door and welcomes visitors.

I adore the Hamptons. It's one of my favorite places on earth, and I feel very lucky to have a summer home there. This private retreat, tucked away in a bucolic area of Long Island, is my escape from the city. I love the fresh farm produce that I can pick up when I want to cook at home, and the unique restaurants for when I don't. I adore the quiet beaches and the little towns and the farms. I even used to have my own store there in a charming shingled cottage on Main Street in Westhampton Beach. But most of all, I'm mad about the lighting. There's something about the way the light shines on things in the Hamptons that's different from any other place I've ever been. Winslow Homer and Jackson Pollock both painted here. Willem de Kooning found inspiration here as well. I am in good company.

My house was built in the 1970s in a modernist way that was popular in the Hamptons at the time. From the outside, it resembles a bunker. Inside, it's very modern, fashioned on three levels with rooms that open into one another. There's no fixed living room, dining room, or library, so I decided to make everything multifunctional. Could a dining room have a desk? Could an entryway have a dining chair? In this house, the answer is yes. It's a free-flowing space with a unique floor plan. I stuck with the architecture of the house as it was. That was a conscious decision on my part, and one you always need to make when you move into a house. Unless it's a brand-new build done to your specifications, you need to face facts and decide whether you're going to live with something or spend time and money making architectural changes to better suit your needs. I'm happy I decided to leave it alone and concentrate instead on a complete decorating job.

How do these two chairs go together? You might as well ask how two very different people get along at a party!

I try to always be willing to take a chance, move beyond my comfort zone, and try new things. This house lets me take design risks. My collection of large cast-plaster sculptures of Roman figures lives in these spaces quite nicely. I love the sense of scale! Most are from the late nineteenth century and early twentieth century. They were in sad shape when I bought them, but I had them restored within an inch of their lives. I also collect pencil drawings of sculptures. I found most of the drawings in London and placed them in antique frames to give them special prominence. It's a nice way to remind myself of the very intellectual and involved process of making art, and all the creative thought that goes into it. I find it very inspirational.

It took some time to figure out the right way to approach the design. At first, I thought I would make it all groovy with intense color. But then I rethought everything and went in a completely different direction. I wanted this to feel like my home, to represent who I am. I went through my inventory of things I already owned, things that really mattered to me, and

If you're having a party, you want to invite a diverse group to make it lively and interesting. I feel the same way about furniture. These chairs—an upholstered Adrian Pearsall modern wing chair and a Guglielmo Ulrich zebra-skin chair—talk to each other in their own way. The rug is like Josef Albers's Homage to the Square. Like almost everything in my house, it's custom made. On the wall, vintage Fornasetti plates with images of Adam hang together. FOLLOWING SPREAD: This den's quiet tones of gray, black and white would be just as at home in New York City. The art deco daybed was originally created for my late partner Bill Diamond's house but now it is with me. The gray cashmere felt fabric is so fabulous. The wood arms of my Adrian Pearsall wing chair are monogrammed and covered with a masculine patchwork fabric of wool suiting fabric.

"My home is a playground for creativity."

settled on a cosmopolitan Roman-holiday feel. It's a country house that's not at all like a country house— it's very masculine, filled with the things that are near and dear to me. I have a memory attached to every single one of the items that now sits in my house. That's part of what a house should be—especially the house of a decorator.

As much as I adore red and gravitate to bright colors, I had the idea that I wanted this house to be kind of chill. I chose a color palette of camel, gray, black, and white. This house is my idea of neutral. Of course, the cheetah prints, stripes, and geometric wallpapers are not everyone's idea of neutral, but this is what I find restful. And we design our homes to please ourselves.

Besides the Roman theme, there are animal prints and likenesses in every room. I always include a little wildlife in my decorating schemes. In this house, animal prints are particularly appropriate because they mirror my color choices. In nature, there is a lot of black and white, chocolate and white, tans, and camels. I covered my '50s-style Harvey Probber sofa with a silk-velvet leopard-print pattern. I have a zebra-skin chair. I used faux-giraffe fabric on a tall wing chair.

I'm lucky enough to have multiple homes. One in Virginia is classically early American. Another in New York City is pop art. And here on Long Island, I honor my Italian roots with Italian-designed modern furniture and classical sculptures and art. My homes are not for everybody, and they will never be trendy. Always go for what you love and what you're comfortable with.

A brass trinket from India sits on my mod, boomerang-shaped cast-terrazzo coffee table. My house is like a travelogue. Wherever I go, I make sure to find a unique decorative item that I can stash in my bag and bring home. I can take that trinket with me to my other homes, too. The table, however, weighs a ton. It's not going anywhere!

A classical nude plaster form— nicknamed Spike— strides through the living room. He embodies confidence. A white leather pouf could work as seating or a coffee table. The rooms and furnishings in this open-floor-plan house need to be multifunctional. The Harlequin lamp is a jolly addition to the room; I found him at an antiques show. When I first bought him, no one knew what he was. Now these Marbro lamps have become quite popular.

OPPOSITE: **The black-and-white pillows look like a loose Matisse drawing of a Roman man. As I've mentioned, Matisse is my favorite artist. Somehow he feels right at home on a leopard sofa. RIGHT: The back of a standing mirror becomes artwork, using decorative marquetry to form Arnold Schwarzenegger from a pattern of wood pieces. It's very captivating. I purchased the zebra suitcase in the early '90s and it has been a part of many interiors of mine. For some odd reason, there's always a place for it in one of my homes! I love it.**

Arts & Crafts
in Venice

THE WORLD IN VOGUE

PREVIOUS SPREAD: The dining room table becomes a grand library table with my collection of art books. I can never have enough. I stack up my old favorites where I can look at them time and time again, and find a place for the new books that I'm excited to display. This is an ever-changing tablescape. Every time I think I get it right, I change it around again. The table is a kind of staging ground for my brain. LEFT: My giraffe chair, like the giraffe itself, stands head and shoulders above other chairs with its super-high back. The painting on the wall feels very old-world but—surprise!—it's a fake. Not everything has to be priceless period art to be valuable. True confession: when I bought it, I thought it was real. But you should know that I don't like it any less now that I know it's not. OPPOSITE: The bed in the master bedroom is custom made from two Victorian sofas that I had re-covered in palomino leather. The side table is from my collection of Belgian Congo Deco-style pieces. I love the geometry of the backgammon pattern and camel-colored leather top, as well as the windowpane pattern on the walls that looks like graph paper.

FOUR FEARLESS DECORATING IDEAS

WHEN IN DOUBT, KEEP IT. I put things I can't use right now in storage. I don't throw things out. There are things I collected when I was much younger that you can't find anymore. They would be very hard to replace. I don't like to part with anything because you never know when it's going to appeal to you again. You might find a new way to make it shine in a different space or a different house. If it's valuable, keep it. If it's re-coverable, re-cover it. These things have character. They are part of your life. Keep them close by. Hopefully you have a big attic or basement!

CHOOSE COLORS THAT LOOK GOOD ON YOU. Have you ever thought about your home the way you do about your clothes? You should! When decorating your home, ask yourself, Does it go with my coloring? Does it fit with my look? Is it my style? I think I look good in my house. I think the colors I chose for my furnishings and walls look good with my coloring and my hair. You want to look good and feel good in your own home.

EVEN DESIGNERS NEED DESIGNERS. With all my knowledge of design, when it comes to my own home, I like to have another designer's eye on it. There are so many decorating decisions to be made when designing a house, and countless ways that it can all come together. When you are doing design work for someone else, you have more emotional distance and it's easy. When it's your own space, it's harder. My creative director, Erick Espinoza, helped me with this project. He doesn't have the same attachments as I do, and he is better able to step back and see the pieces and the spaces as they really are. If you're trying to do your home alone, get help—even if it's from a friend with good taste.

I found this English easel in the basement of an antiques store in London. I remember the day so well. I even remember what I was wearing when I bought it. Every piece of furniture and decoration in this house has a story and is a part of my life.

REPEAT MOTIFS OR THEMES YOU LIKE THROUGHOUT YOUR DECORATING. There's a lot going on in these rooms, but there are unifying themes tying it all together. First, of course, there is the simplified color palette that does not change. Then there is the classical male form, repeated in sculptures, drawings, and on decorative plates. And finally, there are the African animal forms appearing everywhere from end tables to chair coverings to decorative ceramic statues. Echoes of each idea ripple throughout the space.

JOIE DE VIVRE

The couple who lives in this exquisite California home amid stately gardens are the most wonderful hosts. The level of care they take when they open their doors to others is very special. They have a certain way of life that's unique and beautiful. I did everything I could to celebrate that spirit by designing a house that would make their guests feel truly welcome and indulged.

To do so, I turned to the French countryside for inspiration, specifically, settling on and designing everything in an elegant blue-and-white color scheme reminiscent of the Provençal countryside. The result: a splendid home that could as easily be found in Provence as in Los Angeles. I like the idea of decorating everything with blues, because it makes you feel very much like you are in the French countryside. In the living room, soaring ceilings are hung with crystal chandeliers, and baroque windows delight with their playful, sunlit shapes. Intricate floral prints and a blue-and-white gingham check on matching side chairs make guests feel right at home. Grand needn't be synonymous with cold.

I was influenced by the Château de Groussay, a marvelous castle in Montfort-l'Amaury, France, that I had visited. Located west of Paris, it oozes chic, but in the most mannerly way. Many people refer to it as "the other Versailles" because of its wonderful gardens. Similarly, this home has an incredible location and abundant outdoor gardens. This is not just a house, this is a compound; it's a palatial, serene estate, tucked away from the hustle and bustle of Hollywood life. Here, you enter a whole different world. You may even feel like you need to have your passport stamped!

I let my imagination run wild and added some unexpected outbuildings, each one tailored to the lifestyle of the owners.

Inside the dining pavilion, a blue-and-white palette reigns supreme. Two dignified stone lions sit on the mantel of the French limestone fireplace, a nod to the classic sculptures typically found overseeing Parisian gardens. The delightful dining chairs are custom made with a blue-and-white tapestry on the seats and backs.

LEFT: A round burbling fountain invites guests to the French-style dining pavilion, inspired by the Tartar tent at the Château de Groussay. The open, windowed outbuilding, complete with an airy cupola, is surrounded by soaring Italian cypress trees. The surrounding double steps give this small pavilion an architectural boost and an added sense of grandeur and majesty. The rosy terra-cotta roof feels down-to-earth, warm, and welcoming. OPPOSITE: The high ceiling helps the design to soar. Look up at the interior of the cupola, painted blue, and it's like a peek at the California sky. A surprisingly casual American touch is sprinkled in with the addition of the little blue-and-white gingham shades on the chandelier. Life should not be taken too seriously!

Blue and gold are a regal combination that exude quiet grandeur.

Because they do a lot of entertaining, I couldn't help but think of the fabulous Carlos de Beistegui, a mid-twentieth-century Spanish-French interior decorator well known for his entertaining skills. He hosted lavish events attended by the likes of Cecil Beaton, Aga Khan, and Gene Tierney. I wanted all the buildings we worked on to fit that fantasy.

The property is expansive, and there was lots of room for me to play. The freestanding dining pavilion allows for a unique, celebratory way to host guests. And the space itself is versatile: the family can serve dinner in the main house and then invite guests to the pavilion for dessert. Depending on the intimacy of the event, the hosts can set up several round tables or one long banquet table. It can also become a dance floor at a moment's notice. With the right lighting and decor, it can even change into a groovy disco. The interior walls of the pavilion have blue-and-white tiles imported from Portugal in a magical pattern that is elegant and courtly.

Beyond the dining pavilion, there is an outdoor movie theater, a pool house, a guesthouse, and a garden kitchen. The greenhouse kitchen is a favorite of mine and a really fun addition. I love its freestanding nature and how perfectly it is suited to its garden location. There's so much life to it. Guests can be seated and served outside, or they can become part of the action in the kitchen. The hosts like to throw cooking parties where everyone is involved in the meal preparation. It's a particularly wonderful setup because the fresh herbs and vegetables can be plucked from the tended gardens right outside. One of my favorite touches inside the kitchen is the églomisé, or reverse-painted

Louis XV style rules the day in this magnificent hallway, which can't help but impress. A long, low bench with royal blue cushions and gold flourishes is a regal addition. The stone floor? The tall prints? Stately. FOLLOWING SPREAD: Big baroque windows let light into this very formal, grand room. Pretty floral prints have French flair but note that I also used blue and white gingham, which feels very country. The faux marble columns handpainted by Pierre Finkelstein steal the show.

Outdoors, the greenery invites and shelters, encouraging exploration.

glass. It has the most intricate pattern and is reflective of all the nature around it. You see it used throughout Europe, and I knew it would be right at home here. The counters in the kitchen are made in France of lava stone with a custom color applied. The fireplace is French limestone. Blue-and-white tiles dress up the floor beneath the blonde wood table where the epicureans would dine.

The attention to detail continues all the way to the porte cochere. Why leave a typically unused space undecorated or unattended? Guests drive through this entry, and I wanted the feeling of being formally greeted and entertained to start right here. This porte cochere is as delightful as any other area of the property. French finials line the walls for an added flourish.

Of course, none of this could be accomplished without incredible landscape design by Perry Guillot. It's easy to lose yourself in the fantasy created here by tall cypress trees, tidy boxwoods, and manicured holly bushes.

In the end, everything came together in grand and glorious fashion. The blue-and-white Provençal color theme is sweet perfection. Golds and reds grace the interiors with an almost regal air. The deep greens of the lovely lawns and gardens are wholly satisfying. This is a wonderful, tranquil place to call home.

Arched trellises on pillars hung with lanterns lead the way through the gardens while providing shade.

California weather makes it a pleasure for guests to stroll the grounds.

The kitchen pavilion is a wonderful mix of glass and terra-cotta that beckons those wandering the nearby paths to enter—especially if they're hungry! Just follow the warmly inviting stone path. The building is surrounded by gardens that provide fresh herbs and vegetables for culinary creations. FOLLOWING SPREAD: The unique greenhouse kitchen is one of my favorite pavilions on the property. The French limestone floors are dressed up with inlaid blue and white tiles. The counter is pyrolave, a lava stone that can be enameled with incredible custom-made colors. I chose a bright, sea glass green. Matching green cafe chairs surround the large, wood table.

RIGHT: **Even the most functional of spaces, like a porte cochere, can be amped up and made interesting. I thought of it like an art gallery, and I hung antique French finials from the eighteenth and nineteenth centuries on the walls. Then I added lanterns for lighting.**
FOLLOWING SPREAD: **The grand view over the pool and the guest house makes you feel as if you have been transported to the South of France. The tailored mix of cypress trees and boxwoods and wisteria and lavender smells wonderful. The plantings are very particular—notice there are no palm trees. This is an organized, deliberate look. Structured and sculptured. If God were designing a garden in heaven, this would be it.** PAGES 154-155: **Southern California is so conducive to outdoor living. You can create magnificent outdoor rooms with furniture typically reserved for indoor use. The family spends time on this lounge-y, casual porch every day, surrounded by an ever-changing parade of colorful flowers. French limestone floors, an antique limestone fireplace, and limestone Doric pillars help the space feel cool on even the hottest days.**

FOUR FEARLESS DECORATING IDEAS

BRING IDEAS HOME FROM YOUR TRAVELS. Traveling is so important for inspiration. Whenever I am somewhere new, I take a ton of pictures. This magnificent home could not be possible without a deep love and understanding of French country decorating, Portuguese tiles, British stonework, Italian gardens, and more. That comes from firsthand knowledge of the many architectural beauties and decorating delights to be found throughout Europe. Naturally, what I see on my trips weaves its way into my creative visions and I draw upon that when I am back home.

FILL EVERY SPACE WITH FLOWERS. The main house is always filled with buds and blooms, and they embrace you with their beauty and fragrance. I love that! Not all decor is meant to last. Fresh flowers are some of the most wonderful room accessories. They immediately add color and a sense of life. The gardens around the house are full of lush greens, wonderful reds, and deep blues. Because of flowers' temporary nature, don't worry about whether they match the room's palette. An unexpected floral color can be what makes a room come alive.

ADD SCALE WITH WINDOWS. Never underestimate the power of architectural elements like windows when renovating a house. In the double-height living room, I designed the theatrical windows on a big scale. This is a very formal room. The windows needed to match that grandeur. Inspired by Italian mansions, the oversize baroque shapes transport you to another place and time.

IF YOU LIKE IT, USE IT. Have you ever been told that something you like has gone out of style? Ignore that. Clients often get frightened of things that may no longer be on trend. Not me. If I like something, I stick with it. You should, too. Take, for example, the faux marble on the columns in the living room. It works perfectly in this grand room. I can't think of anything I would rather have done there. Classic beauty like this never goes out of style.

LEFT: The poolside pergola, surrounded by carefully manicured holly bushes, provides a necessary shady retreat from the Southern California sunshine. With its cool limestone floor and wooden beams wrapped in lush vines, it is an intensely inviting spot, made more so by the happy buckets of blue hydrangeas and other plants. The teak furniture brings comfort and casual style to a very formal garden setting. The addition of jaunty blue stripes on the sofa and hanging curtains feels at once celebratory and special.

THE CHILL FACTOR

The home's entry feels downright woodsy with a wood-grain wallpaper and durable engineered-wood floor. The pretty hanging lights that line the way are spaceship-esque, and the long runner is a complex circuit board of dynamite colors. The pillows on the leather settee mirror the checkerboard design of the tall cabinet and tease a taste of the color-blocked wall to come one flight down in the living room. Tall pussy willows bring a little of the outside in. FOLLOWING SPREAD: The color-blocked wall in a Mondrian style sets the room apart and shows off the bold palette used throughout the rest of the house.

Downhill skiing can be wild and exciting—an adrenaline rush. Shouldn't a ski condo in Vermont match that level of pulse-racing fun with its own thrills? That's why I thought this retreat, used by an active family with four teens, needed to be designed with a high exhilaration factor. And to me, that meant using big, beautiful blocks of color! It was a clever way to give what was originally a straightforward condo a lot of style.

Of course, I didn't hold back. I enthusiastically created intensely patterned decor. The living room was the main place where I pulled out all the stops, playing with Mondrian-like geometric walls and filling the space with fearless color. Bright shades make perfect sense for the location. Through every window, the outside view is a wintery paradise—and a blank slate. Against that snowy backdrop, the interior wakes you up with a contrasting riot of bold hues and patterns. Why not take it a step further and pair the bright geometric wall with a boldly striped rug of bright blues? Many others would opt for a solid floor covering, but it's good to mix things up in new and different ways. The owners wanted their ski retreat to be happy and colorful, and I was all for that.

The five-bedroom vacation home is built into the side of a mountain for ski-in, ski-out adventures. You enter on the second floor, then descend one flight to the living room. This makes the living room feel more like an old-fashioned rec room, the perfect place to cozy up after a day on the slopes, sip hot chocolate, and play board games. At the same time, this was never going to be a home for people who like to sit around. Everything had to be super durable. Family and friends would be trekking inside with ski boots, trailing wet hats and gloves behind them. I wanted this family to fully enjoy their time

RIGHT: **Downstairs, a gray baby Eames chair and a solid sofa in the living area lend simplicity to busy, eye-catching decor.**
OPPOSITE: **The lines of the furniture are all very clean. It's the colors and fabrics and design that add the boldness. The striped rug is happy and colorful, the perfect scale for a big room. A coffee table made of twigs is pure fun. It's nice to add something that's different while at the same time reflective of Vermont and the great outdoors.**

LEFT: Over the dining room table, I placed a chandelier I like to call "Sputnik in a box." It has a lot of unique style. Think of it as midcentury-modern meets the Jetsons! The wooden Cherner chairs in the dining room have deep blue seats and backs, a perfect match to the vibrant wall behind the buffet. Blue is a wonderful color to use in a home that is surrounded by snow-covered hills. OPPOSITE: In the kitchen, a stone fireplace is a true centerpiece, offering warmth and beauty.

A ski house can be supercool— bold and modern, but still rustic.

skiing, without any fussiness, so I skipped expensive wood flooring and delicate furnishings. Instead, I opted for a more durable engineered composite wood on the floors. Comfy midcentury-modern furniture added to that easy style, but I paired it with items of unexpected scale and materials. In the entry, for example, a trim Hans Wegner love seat is a surprising partner to a massive brown-and-white checkerboard cabinet. There's delight in the way these two pieces can balance and play off each other.

The dining room is open to the kitchen, a wonderful floor plan for a group that values togetherness and wants to bond over their meals. Naturally I chose to go bright, not bland. A lot of people are afraid of color in the kitchen, which is a shame. You don't need to go overboard. Just painting the island a rich blue added the perfect amount of pop the room needed and pulled the color from the dining room wall into the kitchen.

After all the bright oranges and blues of the living areas, I knew I had to soften the palette. In the master bedroom, I opted for soothing tones of beige, making the room an adult retreat in a house full of family and friends. And as I moved into the other bedrooms, the palette expanded to plums and greens.

People often play it safe in ski houses. I'm not sure why, because there's no reason to choose standard fare. I'm not decorating to be staid, and you shouldn't either. A ski condo is a playhouse! That's why having a sophisticated mix of graphic patterns works so well here. It grabs your attention right away, and it says *unbridled happiness* to me.

You can't think Vermont woods and not think plaid. This cozy fabric on the wall adds texture and style. A simple round mirror banded in black provides a neutral counterpoint, and a sense of delight prevails throughout. Everyone gets a kick out of playful touches, like these antler wall sconces set in vintage snowshoes. It's important to add something unexpected in along with the more classic midcentury-modern pieces.

A wool, windowpane wallcovering in the spacious master bedroom has a subdued color but a lively style. A similar but smaller pattern is repeated on the bed, creating a quiet retreat after an active day with friends. The natural bamboo blinds start at the ceiling, above the window. This gives the feeling of additional height, creating an architectural boost for the room. Sleek wood furniture calms the soul, while a gold sunburst mirror above the bed says it's time to rise and shine and hit the slopes again.

LEFT: The bathroom has frosty slivers of marble adorning the wall, which are paired with a gray-and-white geometric wallpaper and a very contemporary wood-veneer vanity.
OPPOSITE: Green plaid on the walls in the guest room feels so toasty and welcoming in this wintry environment. It reminds me of a favorite flannel shirt. And of course, we added a couple of groovy pillows for color and comfort.

The kids' bunk room is one of my personal favorites. The plum-colored linen wallcovering adds texture, and it easily kills the antiseptic nature of the Sheetrock wall beneath. I'm obsessed with the bunk beds themselves, which are made of beautiful bent plywood and inspired by the Scandinavian designer Alvar Aalto. The blonde color of the wood gives it a light and youthful vibe—not at all stodgy. Animal-print pillows are an entertaining reminder of nature and the outdoors.

F. SCOTT FITZGERALD   THE GREAT GATSBY

ERNEST HEMINGWAY   The Old Man and the Sea

Truman Capote   In Cold Blood

F. SCOTT FITZGERALD   TALES OF THE JAZZ AGE   PENGUIN CLASSICS

SENDAK   WHERE THE WILD THINGS ARE   HARPER COLLINS

diane arbus.   An Aperture Monograph

BASQUIAT   HATJE CANTZ

FOUR FEARLESS DECORATING IDEAS

CELEBRATE THE COLORS YOU LOVE. If you have a favorite red or blue or yellow, you'll want to use it somewhere in your house. It will be like an ongoing gift to yourself. If you are working with a designer, show them the shades you love. The owner of this ski condo had a scarf with a swirl of beautiful shades, including plums and greens. She gravitated toward these colors and was hoping to see them in our decor. I loved them too, and I thought they would look perfect in the guest bedrooms and bunk room. We were able to use them to great effect.

BE BOLD AND THINK BIG. There is strength in the scale of the forms you choose. An oversize brown-and-white checkerboard wardrobe commands attention in the entryway. A large chandelier in the dining room has strong lines that give it as much presence as the table under it. Simple Italian cane chairs in a hallway take on new interest when the proportions are elongated and the backs are high. You add a little touch of *Alice in Wonderland* whimsy to the mix when you play with size.

CHOOSE A DESIGN THAT GROWS WITH CHILDREN. Even when there are young ones in the house, it's a mistake to do anything too juvenile. Bunk rooms can easily get campy and kooky with skis and teddy bears. While that can be cool in the short term, children grow very quickly, and you'll have to redecorate the room before you know it. I elevated the bunk room to something more sophisticated, designing it with teens and young adults in mind.

CONSIDER THE PRACTICAL. Houses are meant to be lived in. Think about how the spaces will be used. Do you spend a lot of time in the kitchen? Is there going to be a constant parade of guests? Do you need extra storage in the living room? A designer must take all these things into account. The color-blocked wall unit in the living room has many practical advantages—it hides air-conditioning ducts and beams while also providing storage. The composite-wood floors stand up to high traffic. And faux-wood wallpaper in the entry is much less expensive than planking the walls with the real thing, but it still gives a true sense of quality to the home.

A handsome carved-wood lamp with a large white shade references the Vermont woods as it sits atop a dark brown dresser in the bunk room. I like using different textures such as these to add quality and style to a room. The raindrop mirror by Curtis Jeré adds yet another element to the mix. Its unique, artisanal form lights up the wall.

PRETTY IN PINK

Walk through the doors of this sprawling Manhattan apartment and you enter a wonderland where everything is charmingly pretty and pink. This cotton-candy swirl of a place might not be what you expect to find in a fast-paced urban setting, but that's what makes it such a dream to come home to. It's a fantasy retreat for the clients who live here. I've done two homes for this wonderful couple previously, so we had a great relationship and there was a lot of trust between us. That means there was room for boundless creativity and imagination on everyone's part. In case you can't guess by looking at the pictures, the clients' favorite colors are pink and blue. I took that scheme and ran with it, adding black and white for balance and thereby creating something akin to Paloma Picasso's apartment in Paris in the 1970s. What can I say? It's like a piece of French pastry. It's yummy!

This was such an exciting project for me. It was a complete renovation, and I was involved in every inch of the rooms, which is what I like best. I started by suggesting changes to many architectural features of the apartment. For example, the living room was quite large, but had no real interest or focal point. We added a grand fireplace with a lovely mantel and classic arches to that room, and suddenly a long, somewhat plain space was transformed and the room had a focus. The decor came together quickly after that. Working from the ground up, I installed a giant rug that looks like a Pucci scarf. Fashion for the floor! All those incredible swirls keep everything light and lyrical. The pastel-pink French Deco upholstered furniture has an intentionally feminine vibe—so deliciously delicate and beautiful.

In juxtaposition to the comfy seating and the lush fabrics, I used a lot of sparkling blue glass as decorative touches. It has a

The kitchen is smooth and cool—like an icy gelato—with lots of white cabinetry, bright blue hues, and soft pink accents. The custom-fitted refrigerator steals the show with its colorful geometric blocks and sleek, mod handles. The plexiglass front is back-painted to achieve this beautiful effect. No one can say it's not one of a kind. Polka dots painted on a black floor illuminate the whole room and offer a pleasing path to all the goodies hidden behind that wall of doors. The seamless countertop is perfection: blue lava stone from France. It's glazed with enamel and has a shiny, crackled finish that you can't get with any other countertop material.

PREVIOUS SPREAD: **This room has an Old Hollywood look. The fireplace was inspired by one that Dorothy Draper designed for an apartment lobby in the 1940s. I'm constantly making references to the decorating greats. It's my way of paying homage to them. Blue-reverse-painted glass is used in the fireplace surround. The fireplace screen is also glass, allowing all the delicate beauty to shine through.** RIGHT: **A pair of tiny pink barrel chairs in the same room as a great big sofa? Yes, please! Changing scale in a room is a surefire way to add personality and style. Keep it loose. Designing and decorating are not exact sciences. The living room "wears" my version of a vibrantly colorful Pucci scarf on its floor. The linked pink fabric appears on the sofa, ottoman, and art deco club chairs, underscoring the monochromatic nature of the room. The bookcase covers an entire wall to house the couple's impressive collection of art books. A painting cleverly conceals a television set hung from the middle of the bookcase. Talk about mixed media!**

LEFT: In the bathroom, I decorated with floor-to-ceiling curtains. The room envelops you in matching fabrics. The shower curtain even matches the vinyl-backed fabric walls. And guess what? Now you are no longer looking at a tub, a shower, a toilet, or a vanity. I don't want to look at those things. It's much nicer to see the pink polka dots take over. OPPOSITE: In the breakfast nook adjacent to the kitchen, another Pucci-inspired rug rules the roost. A 1960s-style Venetian glass chandelier is a heavenly addition that makes the pretty room even prettier. Blue-lacquered walls are my way of tying a bow around this little gift of a room.

There's something unabashedly Parisian about decorating with pink.

cooling effect everywhere throughout the apartment. I used it in the living room, the breakfast nook, the kitchen, and the bathroom. All that exquisite glass feels like spun sugar on the top of an amazing cake. The apartment wouldn't be the same without it.

One look at this pretty palace and you know that Dorothy Draper, the great American designer, is another obvious influence for me. Who isn't captivated by her bountiful use of bright colors and energetic mix of styles and patterns? These days, it's known as the Hollywood Regency style. She loved black in a room, and I love black too. It's very dramatic, especially when it's used with a lot of color, as it is here. The floors in the apartment are all painted black. It's a great way to lay the groundwork for an intensely colorful space. By the way, if the flooring is lackluster in a house, black paint is an excellent choice. It hides many flaws and makes the wood look luxe. Of course, the dark hue didn't stop me from playing games. In the kitchen, for example, I added colorful polka dots to the floor with a hand-painted design inspired by British artist Damien Hirst.

In fact, the kitchen is one of the most spectacular rooms in the apartment. Many kitchens these days are too high-tech and fashion-y for my taste. I know it's easy to get sucked into whatever the latest trend is and to want all the latest gadget wizardry, but I try to stay with the basics. We started with simple white wood-and-glass cabinetry. Then we jazzed up the fridge and glass cabinets, because it was time for some excitement. The mosaic-style, reverse-painted plexiglass gives it a playful beauty. It's a statement piece that's perfectly reflective of the project's palette. To top it off, the counter in front of the refrigerator is a luscious deep-blue lava stone. The round, white egg-crate table topped with glass is a visual delight reminiscent of the work of Gio Ponti. The whole room is full of surprises. I don't say this about many kitchens, but I think I could live in this one.

The entire apartment has a fun vibe. When you go in, you just want to smile. That's the reaction I look for when I decorate. I don't want you to walk in and say, "Ooh, this is so sophisticated," even if it is. I want you to walk in and simply say, "I'm happy here."

Everyone loves a bright and shiny white kitchen. The cabinetry I chose is simple and sophisticated. A row of tall glass cabinets above the countertop add light and style. A single gooseneck faucet is elegant, and the stainless steel stove keeps everything fresh. The blue walls of the breakfast nook area extend into the kitchen to tie the two spaces together.

This pretty apartment is purposely full of sensual curves. The white island counter furniture takes on a delightfully fluid, feminine shape that is repeated in the white chair backs. As a counterpoint to so many whimsical and curvy elements, the blue settee in the hallway is squared off and angular. The definitive black-and-white striped walls provide a balance to the sweet and sugary swirls of blues and pinks in the Pucci-style carpet beneath.

The bedroom is a pink dream. Sometimes you just have to jump right in and spin a cocoon of color. Everything in the bedroom is the same rose-petal hue, at the request of the clients. It's like cotton candy. Or the inside of a seashell. These clients wanted to be surrounded by a color they loved. Can I say I was tickled pink to do it for them? How many chances do you get as a designer to do an all-pink room? The pattern on the carpet is similar to the one on the chairs in the living room, and all the shapes are curvy and soft.

FOUR FEARLESS DECORATING IDEAS

START A BOOK COLLECTION. Of course, there are books, books, books everywhere in this apartment. I wanted to showcase the couple's collection of great titles. I don't think I've ever done a house without a bookcase. As far as I'm concerned, it's not a home without one. I advise all young people to start collecting early. Pick up catalogs from museums you visit. Buy fashion books. Bring home books on interior design. Treasure your art books. And don't forget novels! They are an important part of your collection, too. Surround yourself with books the way you do with other well-loved items. Display them, read them, share them.

USE ONE COLOR THROUGHOUT TO MAKE A SPACE LOOK BIGGER. I've done a lot of one-color rooms over the years, but this was the first time I did one that was all pink. I loved it so much that I know it won't be the last. When you use the same shade over and over in one room, something interesting happens. The eye is tricked into thinking the space is bigger than it is. Of course, you must feel strongly about a color to take this giant step. Be sure you're fully committed. A one-color room envelops you in a positive way, creating a buffer from the outside world. It's a little like being in our own personal bubble.

LET YOURSELF BE SURPRISED. Good decorating is not rigid or regimented. Your home should never end up looking like a tidy little show house when completed. It's the surprises in decorating that make for a fun room and a place that feels good to live in. A well-decorated space should be the result of the natural ways in which we talk, live, entertain, eat, and relax in our own private spaces. Maybe a chair gets pulled in for a conversation one day, and you realize it's best kept that way. Keep your options open. Move things around until they please you.

BUY THREE MAJOR PIECES AND THEN WAIT FOR THE MAGIC TO START. Many people feel overwhelmed by the idea of decorating a whole apartment or house. If you are nervous about how it will all come together, start small. Buy three main pieces that you truly love. Maybe you find an amazing antique chair, a hand-painted chest, and a handsome grandfather clock. It's OK to stop there for a beat. Wait. Live with the pieces for a while. Get to know them. Let them sit until the plan starts to emerge by itself.

Details are undeniably important, and they make for a complete and compelling design. Even the doors to the wardrobe deserve to be part of the show. We had them hand-painted with the same lively and fluid scarf theme that appears in the living room and breakfast nook. Pop-art swirls of black, white, blue, and pink burst from the wall, and an adjacent door leads to the blue-tiled master bathroom.

SEASIDE SPLENDOR

The entry is done in a calm sand color that reminds me of the string of beaches that line the Hamptons. The rug is a subdued hue, but it boasts a great big geometric pattern—like Chinese fretwork, blown up big. The benches flanking the wide hallway are actually meant for garden use, but I love placing them indoors. A neat pair of bow-front chests lends a dignified profile.

This big Shingle Style Hamptons home is one of quiet sophistication, all wrapped up in a pretty blue bow. There are shades of the sea everywhere—what better color for a home located a mere block from the Atlantic Ocean? At the same time, this seaside mansion is a far cry from a simple beach house. It speaks to a more refined life of quiet afternoons, evening cocktail parties, formal dinners, and late-night stargazing. To that end, I chose to incorporate serene coastal colors without making the decor feel overly beachy. The color palette we ultimately chose reflects the rich natural environment of the Hamptons: ocean blues, gray-greens, sand colors, emerald greens, and darker, deeper blues. The woodwork is bright, fresh, and mainly white, and the home is perfectly suited to its location, both inside and out. The Shingle Style exterior is very much in sync with the fashionable interior.

I knew the house needed to be elegant but not stuffy, because it would be both a weekend getaway and the summer base of operations for a sporty family. They're often golfing and playing tennis at a nearby country club, but they return home to rest, relax, and entertain. There are five inviting bedrooms for accommodating extended family.

The property is situated on an inland pond, affording the house lovely water views from almost every window downstairs and ocean views from the top floor. The architectural plan called for special windows to be used everywhere—pretty decorative ovals and rounds, plus transom windows, French windows, and bay windows. Sunshine fills the house and reminds you constantly of what is waiting for you outdoors.

As you reach the top of the stairs, you arrive at a winning spot for quiet reflection. The landing links two wings of the house, but before you decide which way to go, you might want to take a book from the shelves that encircle this space and sit for a few moments. A round table in the center is the perfect place for a collection of pretty art books and a bursting bouquet of summer flowers. The blue ceiling is a high point, drawing the eye up as you ascend the stairs and providing a sky-like canopy for those who stop to enjoy it.

Time slows down with a grand, sweeping staircase.

The house is also a showcase for the clients' extensive collection of art and antiques. They have been collecting and curating things over the years that were found on various buying trips. I've done other houses for these clients before, and I was familiar with a lot of their choices—I had even been with them for many of their purchases. When clients and a designer go shopping together, you learn a lot about one another. We added to the things they already had for this house with an additional trip to London for some new discoveries. The grandfather clock was the first new item we bought specifically with this residence in mind. It became so central to the plan for the entry that we created a special architectural niche for it. Because this was a new build, I was able to confer with the architect and act as a team—designer, architect, and clients—to do things like that.

Many of the public spaces are unusually generous, such as the wide entry hall and the double-height landing on the second floor. The landing is big enough to also act as a library and sitting area. These spaces add a pleasantly decorous touch to the house, giving the feeling that time slows down here. The house feels like a throwback to a more courteous and compassionate time, when you were at your leisure to sit quietly with a book, enjoy lively conversation, or simply admire the keepsakes and photos on display.

The living room has a reserved British air, with its monochromatic blue-gray tones. The fantasy of this room is the big double-height windows. Thanks to two fireplaces and two separate seating areas, this room can easily handle a

A staircase can make or break a house. It can add incredible beauty to a home or take it away. This one curves grandly upward in a classic shell-like sweep. I didn't want the pretentiousness of the double staircase that I see in some large American country estates. The staircase is old-school with an elegant patterned runner and white banister. The classic seaside compass motif on the ground floor was achieved with different wood stains. FOLLOWING SPREAD: In a big double height room like this it is important to pay as much attention to the architecture as the decorating. To that end, we have fabulous round windows, gorgeous paneled walls, clerestory windows, and huge pine mantels. I love the mix of natural wood color and paint. I chose a monochromatic look, using a blue-gray-green throughout.

Don't underestimate the pretty power of quiet, gracious elegance.

crowd. As formal as the living area may be, however, it is also extremely inviting. I am a stickler about having big, plush couches in family homes. I used a wide blue-and-white stripe to turn the formality of the room down a notch, making it a more congenial place to sit. The fabric reminds me of a cheerful beach umbrella.

The house features gracious arches throughout, from the living room to the kitchen to the bedroom. Arches are part of my lexicon. They work well in a traditional house, adding style and lyricism. The colors and patterns and furnishings here are all timeless. I think this family will never tire of the design. The clients like a very tailored look, which we achieved, but at the same time there's a sense of casualness and comfort, too. They want to be relaxed and have fun entertaining friends. I was able to achieve that balance for them—quiet spaces, lively interiors, dramatic rooms, and free-flowing spaces. To spend time in this house is to spend time truly enjoying life.

Blue-and-white Delft tiles are the perfect companions for a sandy beige rug. A tailored sideboard with delicate legs speaks to an old-world elegance. The window echoes the unusual oval shape of the dining room, and Georgian-style wood lanterns, custom made in London, provide lighting.

The dining room is an oval shape with a series of archways and lots of white woodwork. There's something about the symmetry of this room that is particularly pleasing. The gray-blue chairs are handsome partners to a rich wood table; the room reflects the colors of the Atlantic with its blues, grays, and greens; and the walls are a sandy color.

The kitchen is all white except for the blonde-wood island, and this is a relaxed space where tall windows let in tons of happy sunlight. The blue-and-white geometric rug pattern is taken from a quilt and has a more modern feel than the rest of the house.

Through French doors and clerestory windows, there are fabulous views of the Atlantic Ocean, the inspiration for our color palette of blues.

The room enjoys a grand scale, thanks to its double-height windows and tray ceiling—the extra space was captured from the attic. We really pulled out all the stops with the woodwork in this room: there are neoclassical pediments above the French doors, which open out to a balcony. Through the French doors and the clerestory windows, there are fabulous views of the vast Atlantic Ocean. FOLLOWING SPREAD: The vanity (left) was designed to have a mix of mahogany and paint which creates a very striking look, almost like a line drawing. It automatically kills the boredom of a basic bathroom vanity. On the right, a footed tub is a gracious, classic addition to any large bathroom.

The guest bedroom
has oval elements
repeated throughout.
It's very cool to use
the same form over
and over in one
room. The beds are
custom made from
antique cherry.

Nothing is as important in a summer house as a screened porch. In my opinion, it is a must! The furniture is rattan, both light and substantial at the same time. It's a wonderful space for casual, free-flowing entertainment. The outside trim in blue reminds you that you are only a block from the ocean.

FOUR FEARLESS
DECORATING IDEAS

STATE CLEARLY WHAT YOU WANT. If you are working with a designer, be sure to share your expectations. Go through every category, from color to storage needs. Think ahead. Be specific. For example, say, "I want the wine storage in my kitchen and not in the dining room." If you gather all that knowledge and together put it in a list, you and your designer will avoid those expensive eleventh-hour changes.

IF YOU MAKE A MISTAKE, MAKE A CHANGE. Every once in a while, something you had hoped would look amazing just doesn't. Eliminate it. Don't try to retrofit the problem, hoping you can find a way to live with what you don't like. It will only compound the problem, and you'll still be unhappy in the end. Sometimes, however, the solution is as simple as moving a piece of furniture or a painting from one room to another. Don't think of it as a mistake. It's a happy accident! One of the reasons to keep to a strict palette throughout your house is so you can move things around from room to room this way.

USE ARCHITECTURAL ELEMENTS TO MAKE A HOME MORE INTERESTING. I like the rhythm of the arched shape. Its curves are the anecdote for a stagnant room. They add drama and poetry. I am always drawn to unique woodwork— from columns and pilasters to unusual trim, crowns, vaulted ceilings, and arched windows. Keep it fresh and lively by changing up the woodwork. It doesn't all have to be the same. One door can celebrate natural wood; another can be painted.

MATCH THE EXTERIOR OF THE HOUSE TO THE INSIDE. To be done properly, the decor inside a house must match the facade. Big, modern, open spaces would never work inside a classic Shingle Style house in the Hamptons. Make a conscious decision to help your house stick to its roots. It should be what it was meant to be. In this case, the house was meant to be traditional—with a twist, of course.

The sitting room off the kitchen is one of the many unique and interesting spaces in this giant house. The window is an interior one and looks into a hallway, so I used pebbled translucent glass and then ran deep shelving across it. Next, I gave several sets of identical Delft canisters their marching orders, arranging them in satisfyingly symmetrical rows. Two clubby chairs in white complete the picture.

COLONIAL REVIVAL

The gracious proportions of the rooms in this house are evident in the tall shuttered windows, set deep into thick walls. The house has unusually high ceilings. It was modeled after London townhouses. The lawyer who lived there wanted to show off his wealth with this house. I painted the moldings around the window a deep teal, set off against a contrasting chalky white and a barn red. The result is quite striking. The wide-plank wood floors, so iconic of Williamsburg, add a comfortable warmth to the home.

When the folks at Colonial Williamsburg called and asked me to decorate Palmer House—a brick house built in 1755 near the Capitol Square—as my home, I was delighted. I had visited Colonial Williamsburg as a boy on a family trip and I've always been in love with the place. Williamsburg wasn't just the capital of Virginia in the early 1700s; it was also the center of architecture and decoration, and that period is rightly considered to be a golden age of design. I was asked to be a designer in residence as a way to continue to promote American design efforts, and I am proud to share my design inspiration with those who visit this home.

I was only nine years old on my first trip to Colonial Williamsburg, but I was completely fascinated by all the architectural details in the Governor's Palace such as the crown moldings and window casings. I marveled at the ballroom because of its grand scale. It was the first time I ever saw a tray ceiling. I visited the printer and learned not only about how things were printed, but also the role of journalism in the American Revolution and the importance of free speech in this country. I saw jewelry being designed and watched a blacksmith work his forge.

When I returned to Williamsburg to work on this house, I became reacquainted with the town and saw the majesty of it all—the effort and the joy that goes into creating it. It's such an inspirational place for young people and for everyone, really. It's important to learn where we are from, to experience our history as a young country and the history of American design. Lucky me! I now have a front-row seat to it all.

The large entry hall introduces visitors to everything that is special about this house. A charming mix of collectibles, from a large black pitcher on the steps to mounted models of ships lacquered to a high shine on the walls, speaks to a rich history. The model ships are a reminder that so much of what Colonial Williamsburg has today came in by boat from abroad. The entry hall boasts no less than three amazing wooden chests, one of them hand-painted with colorful flags. They remind me of what a ship's captain might travel with. I use a lot of chests in my decorating; I love them because they spark imagination. What treasures could be inside?

There aren't many patterns in the house—I wanted to keep mainly to solids like the gold settee— but the fabric on the American chair with rolled arms by the window is a winner. Its pattern is inspired by a nineteenth-century American coverlet design. The blue is the perfect color for a Virginia home. My love of American domestic architecture is evidenced here. The patterns are folksy and elegant at the same time. The red braided rug is a classic American handcrafted element.

In the dining room, a vibrant gold plays off the blue wainscoting and white walls. I was influenced by the costumes of the interpreters at Colonial Williamsburg. The strong white, yellow, and blue of their clothing is so simple and so inspiring. The black Windsor chairs are a mix of real and reproductions. None of them match; it's a compiled dining set.

Sometimes I wake up in this house to a fife and drum corps playing in the streets. How cool is that? It's a fantasy living in colonial times, walking on a colonial street.

The concept of the house was that it was to be my house. Not Mr. Palmer's house. He was the gentleman, attorney, and property owner who lived there starting in the 1750s with his wife and daughters. I am the gentleman who lives here in 2019! It was important, however, that the house represent both of us because people come to see the house and tour it. Like the rest of Colonial Williamsburg, it is a living museum, but the emphasis is on the living, not on the museum.

I filled the house with eighteenth-century furniture and eighteenth-century reproductions. There's an idea today that everything has to be an exquisite period piece in order to be worthy, but that's not true. Reproductions can be wonderful if they are well made. During the 1920s, furniture makers created some amazing eighteenth-century revival pieces, such as the highboy dresser I used in one of the bedrooms. And guess what? I got it at an auction for only $500.

For the palette, I wanted to use all primary colors from Benjamin Moore's Williamsburg collection—but not just any primary colors. The concept was to use real colors that they would have used in Williamsburg in the eighteenth century. I wanted to bring back the flavor of the true colonial colors—which is a much brighter palette than one would expect. I chose gold, a blue-gray, and a barn red. These colors suit the house and pull the look together. I used mostly solid upholstery throughout the rooms, veering only occasionally toward a pattern. It was a conscious decision to add my absolute favorites, such as a gingham check on a classic American chair.

I love this house because it shows how we live today—inspired by the past, influenced by the future, and impacted by the world around us.

Instead of using wallpaper, it was more fun to stencil a lattice pattern on the wainscoting. The idea came from another historic Virginia home. Four black-and-white William Hogarth prints on the wall tell wonderful stories. A bust of Napoleon sits on a George Washington desk. Old plaster casts are one of the recurring themes in my homes. FOLLOWING SPREAD: In the master bedroom, the contemporary brass bed comes from Gore Vidal's estate. It's so big that I never had room for it in any of my houses. At last, it found a home! Contemporary touches like this remind you that this historic home is lived in by a modern man. The artwork over the bed is created from a grouping of antique door hinges that form a corona. It originally hung in one of the Williamsburg hotels. The red pillows on the bed are from a house in the Adirondacks. Why not? It all fits. A dark wood chest sits at the foot of the bed.

People don't realize what colonial color is about. They imagine it's dreary and drab but it's quite the contrary: bright and bold and saturated.

Sometimes I like to do a more feminine guest room. I thought I would soften the experience of the house by starting off with salmon pink walls. A pair of dark wood four-poster beds from the Carnegie's summer house looks sweet. The lady's writing desk is part of the collection of the Williamsburg Foundation.

FOUR FEARLESS DECORATING IDEAS

GO AS BIG AS YOU CAN. I hate twee, little things. They are not fearless. Go as big and bold as what will fit through the door. An eight-foot-tall dresser in the right room will look like nothing! I used a great big butter churn as a base for a lamp in one room and a tall antique nineteenth-century sewing box for the base of a lamp in another room. The shades are oversize, too. Let the objects fill the space. Proportion is everything.

COLLECT! COLLECT! COLLECT! Everything old is eventually new again. Start building your history today by keeping the pieces that are important to you and adding to that collection with more items from yesteryear. Time flies by, and modern furniture becomes retro very quickly. Think about it: something from the 1920s is already 100 years old. I may start collecting '90s pieces next. It's nice to see old furniture repurposed and reproduced. It becomes part of the never-ending cycle of design.

A quilt top is used as fabric on the settee in the entry hall. Did I let the fact that the quilt wasn't big enough to cover it stop me? I did not. It was the perfect opportunity to improvise and add to the charm with a second solid fabric on the arms. There are a lot of Dutch influences throughout the house, like this wooden windmill on the wall. So many goods were brought into the colony from Holland and Portugal and beyond. I wanted to reflect that in the decorating.

LOOK FOR A GOOD DEAL. You can walk away with some amazing things at furniture auctions. I am always pleasantly surprised and rarely disappointed. The trick is to reimagine it after you've nabbed it. For example, I got the American Empire settee I used for the living room at an auction for only $200. That's a steal! No one who sees it now—a handsome piece covered in a beautiful gold fabric sitting happily in a Colonial Williamsburg brick house—would believe that.

DON'T LET HISTORY GET IN THE WAY OF MODERNITY. A home is not a stage set. It is a design for living. No matter how traditional or historical your home may be, you want to also include contemporary touches, as I did here. Do not be rigid. Rigidity is not fun or fearless. It only leads to frumpiness.

RED-HOT STYLE

Richie Rich, Dagwood and Popeye used to belong to my friend and partner, the late Bill Diamond. They were his favorites. Fortunately, I came across these pop-art paintings rolled up in a storage unit, I rescued them, and we were reunited! They're an entertaining group to come home to, and they go with my primary color scheme. FOLLOWING SPREAD: The black-lacquered end tables on either side of my bed have been with me for years and multiple homes. Black adds punctuation to any interior, so I almost always have something black in the room.

When I moved into a high-rise in the middle of bustling midtown Manhattan, I saw it as a chance to do something different. My apartment sits way up in the sky, with amazing views of the Hudson River and the city below. One wall of the apartment is a floor-to-ceiling glass window, and the glory of Manhattan is always on full display. It's a nonstop show, with boats moving down the Hudson, lights going on and off, and people bustling about on the streets below.

There's no way to compete with that sight, so I began by painting everything white. Next, I filled my home with what I love. That's what you should do, too. Truly, it's the best advice I can give to anyone who is decorating a home. For me, that means lots of red—on a bedspread, a rug, a chair. Have I mentioned my love affair with that color? Red means so many things, like passion and love and energy. What can't you say with red? I paired that vibrant shade with bright yellow, black, and white. Blue makes an appearance as well, of course—most notably in the mod Kim MacConnel painting that hangs above my bed. His work is bold and colorful and highly patterned; it's an ideal match for me.

It always suits me to have something whimsical and playful in every room. The cabana-style cabinets were one of the first pieces I ever designed, and the pair happily sat in a client's house for close to twenty years before recently coming back to me when those clients moved. Lucky me! I welcomed them home. The striped lamps originally belonged to my sister—I picked them out for her—and now they are back, too. Like most people, I'm happiest when I'm surrounded by things that mean something to me.

I adore retreating to my pied-à-terre in the sky. It's a happy place that is very colorful and graphic. Just my style!

HENRI MATISSE
michelcomte
The Peggy Guggenheim
INTO ACTION
GEORGE PLATT LYNES
FRENCH RIVIERA
LUXURY TOYS

MIAMI
Andy Warhol Portraits
ALBERTO PINTO Classics
HENRI MATISSE
FASHION IN COLORS
SURREAL THINGS

FOUR FEARLESS DECORATING IDEAS

USE WHAT YOU ALREADY OWN. When you move into a new place, the temptation is to go out and buy all new things for it. But that's not necessary, nor is it affordable. Instead, go back and choose among things you have collected over the years. I looked at items that have been with me in previous homes. I don't let go of things easily—a black-and-white cashmere throw a favorite aunt made sits on the back of my chair. And my porcelain zebras from Italy hop around everywhere with me. I make sure the same piece of art or a certain beloved side table reappears. You look at it in a whole new way when it has a fresh placement in a changed environment.

REMEMBER THAT RENTAL SPACES ARE NOT FOREVER. There is a sense of freedom in knowing that your decorating decisions are not set in stone. In a few years, you might be living in a completely different style of apartment or house, and you can do something else with your walls and floors there. Take this opportunity to have a little fun with your furnishings. This can be a time to experiment, to do something you might have been afraid to try before. Knowing that you are allowed to change your mind gives you permission to let your personality shine.

DON'T OVERDO ANY ONE ELEMENT. I love shiny things, and if I weren't careful, I would probably have chrome and lacquer everywhere in my apartment. But I limit myself, and that's why it works so well. Too much of a good thing can be overwhelming. Mix up your mediums. Balance the smooth and sleek with the warm and soft; the curves with the straight edges; the stripes with the patterns. Rooms work much better when they contain a collection of various textures, sizes, and shapes.

IT DOESN'T HAVE TO BE FLAWLESS. Did you notice that my chair is technically too big for the room it's in? Or that I left a painting on the floor rather than hang it up? Of course not. You were too busy enjoying the space. These things are not perfect, and I don't care. That's why they are appealing. The lack of perfection gives a home the looseness it needs. You don't want everything around you to be too "done" and poised. That would feel rigid and boring—trust me. And you want to feel light and happy when you open the door.

OPPOSITE: The stripes of these beachy cabanas are cheerful, and they make what is otherwise a very urban apartment feel friendlier. The glass end table is a copy of a classic Warren Platner table. I like to use glass and chrome in small spaces because they have a light, airy footprint.

To William Diamond—my mentor, my partner, my friend.
Lovers of great design will forever be inspired
by your singular vision. Your work was about joy, and you
succeeded in bringing that joy to so many.

I am thrilled to work with two stars: Jaime Magoon, my senior designer, and Erick Espinoza, my creative director. Three cheers for their youthful inspiration! One of the best ways to continue to grow is to surround yourself with smart young designers. Each one has an unbeatable eye and is highly educated—Jaime went to Rhode Island School of Design, and Erick went to the New York School of Interior Design. Their academic chops, combined with their intense creativity and fine taste, make them who they are.

Thanks to Indrani Doobay, Ahila Shah, and Nilesh Shah for their constant support and energy. You can see our respect for one another in everything we do.

Thanks to my amazing clients, who inspired and trusted me—and whose happy homes are generously shared in this book: Linda and Jim Lippman; Eric and Paula Gleacher; Robin Weingast and Claire Zeppieri; Alan Falcone; Robert and Libby Alexander; Mark and Lori Fife; and Elyssa Kellerman.

Thanks to the incredible artisans with whom I have worked: Adam Lowenbein; Thomas Newman; Kevin Cross; David Osbourne; Gael De Brousse; David Cohn; Lloyd Marks and Michael Tavano; Osmundo Echevarria; Jesse Lopez; Lisa Simkin; Raoul and Julien Benassaya; Lois Chernin; Paul Ferrante; Dora Helwig; Finn Hegner; Bielecky Brothers; Charles H. Beckley; Spencer Tomkins; Ruben and Jimmy Cabrera; Mark Ogrodowicz; Stephen Elrod; Stark Carpet; Karen Rodgers; Tim Sheridan; Anthony Monaco; Pedro Leitao; Cameron Capel; Nancy Reib; Sean O'Connell; Chambord Prints Inc.; Erin Wilson; Sandor Collection; the De Angelis family; Paul Flammang; Phyllis Leck; Jan Jurta; May Yong; Pierre Finklestein; and Maeve Bristow.

Thank you to Giorgio Guidotti, Eric Bremner, Marco Cepparo, and Sara Lodi at Max Mara.

And to the Colonial Williamsburg Foundation—it has been a pleasure and honor to work with you: Jeff Duncan; Kiri Franco; Liza Guzzler; Cheryl Griggs; and Jillian Pyle.

I am grateful for the incredible spirit and vision of my friends at Thomasville Furniture: Regan Iglesia; Reyna Moore; and Skip Rumley.

Thanks to the many talented editors who have featured my work: Clinton Smith; Kendell Cronstrom; Doris Chevron; Doretta Sperduto; Pilar Viladas; Amy Astley; Sophie Donelson; Steele Marcoux; Pamela Jaccarino; and DJ Carey.

To the gifted architects and contractors with whom I have partnered: Arian Myrto; Misha Rakovsky; Don Cantillo; Ricardo Vargas; Steve Giannetti; Tom Ambler; Perry Guillot; Tony Wala of Simply Elegant; Jim and Dick Reeves; Jamie Catley of Kent Construction; and Lee Development Co.

I could not have written this book without the help of: my indefatigable agent, Jill Cohen; my talented partner in writing, Antonia van der Meer; my wonderful editor, Kathleen Jayes; and the inimitable creative team of Doug Turshen and David Huang.

First published in the United States of America
in 2020 by Rizzoli International Publications, Inc.
300 Park Avenue South
New York, NY 10010
www.rizzoliusa.com

Copyright © 2020 Anthony Baratta

Text: Antonia van der Meer

Photography and Art Credits:

Nicholas Baratta: page 9, 13

©Roger Davies/OTTO: pages 137-156

Erick Espinoza: reverse of front endpaper, pages
4, 66, 119-134, 239

Alison Gootee. Images originally appeared
in House Beautiful, a publication of Hearst
Magazine Media, Inc.: pages 233-236

James Merrell: pages 77-94

Keith Scott Morton: pages 97-116, 159-174

©Eric Piasceki/OTTO: pages 15-38

Mark Roskams: pages: 10, 193-214

Annie Schlechter: pages 2, 6, 40-58, 177-190,
217-230, reverse of back endpaper

Kris Tamburello: pages 61-74

Artwork on front cover: Ji Zhou, "The Map,
No. 8," 2016, courtesy of the Eli Klein Gallery

Publisher: Charles Miers
Senior Editor: Kathleen Jayes
Design: Doug Turshen with David Huang
Production Manager: Barbara Sadick
Managing Editor: Lynn Scrabis

All rights reserved. No part of this publication may
be reproduced, stored in a retrieval system, or
transmitted in any form or by any means, electronic,
mechanical, photocopying, recording, or otherwise,
without prior consent of the publisher.

Printed in Italy

2020 2021 2022 2023 / 10 9 8 7 6 5 4 3 2 1

ISBN: 978-0-8478-6682-3

Library of Congress Control Number: 2019950327

Visit us online:
Facebook.com/RizzoliNewYork
Twitter: @Rizzoli_Books
Instagram.com/RizzoliBooks
Pinterest.com/RizzoliBooks
Youtube.com/user/RizzoliNY
Issuu.com/Rizzoli